Harold E Bailey
Trapper

The Friendly Trapper
by Harold E. Bailey

© 1987, 1992, 1994, 1995 by Trapper Publications
Revised 1992, 1994
Revised and expanded in 1995

Published and Printed by:
CITY PRINTING COMPANY
36 West Wood St. • Youngstown, OH 44503

Photography by .... Dan DiThomas
Cover Art by .... Chris Yambar
Illustrations by .... Steve Honthy
Edited by .... Karen Miller

Distributed by: **TRAPPER PUBLICATIONS**
P.O. Box 423 • Canfield, OH 44406–0423 • 216 549–2010

BOOKLAND EAN   MAG 80   LWR 0.7   FilMaster™
Trapper Publications

ISBN 0-9...

D1039298

9 78(

INFINITY 2277 SCIENCE, OKEMOS, MICHIGAN 48864
PHONE 1-800-292-CODE   FAX 1-517-349-7608

TO ALL MY FRIENDS

BOOKLAND EAN   MAG 80   LWR 0.7   FilMaster™
Trapper Publications
INFINITY 2277 SCIENCE, OKEMOS, MICHIGAN 48864
PHONE 1-800-292-CODE • FAX 1-517-349-7608
© 1987, 1992, 1994, 1995 by Trapper Publications

ISBN 0-9644941-0-8

ACKNOWLEDGEMENTS

I am sincerely grateful to all of the people who have gone out of their way to assist me. Also, an expression of appreciation to all those individuals who helped with the compiling, selling, or in any other way contributed to the publication of the expanded and revised version of this book.

And, a very special thank you to my assistant and traveling companion, Elsie. Her dedication, inspiration and loyalty were greatly appreciated. Thank you, my dear wife, who passed away in 1994.

A special word of thanks to friends Ken and Fran Brayer, for without their help this project would never have been possible. To Karen Miller for her editing and encouragement and Mary McGee for her organizational abilities, I will always be grateful. Thanks, to Lorraine A. Brown for all of her special touches and expert advice in completing the set up of this book. Thanks also, to Marie Dornshuld for her many contributions.

GOD BLESS MA AND PA AND MR. BAILEY.

TABLE OF CONTENTS

INTRODUCTION

"The Friendly Trapper", otherwise known as Harold E. Bailey of Columbiana, Ohio is that oracle, and his wisdom reaches vast numbers of people via radio and T.V. Tune in and keep pencil and paper handy not only for household hints and recipes, but for calls to Trapper as he shares his wealth of knowledge.

His face, too, is familiar to countless persons who have watched him gratefully, sometimes from a safe distance as he snared raccoons, bagged hornets' nests, "treated" yellow jackets to a lethal mixture of caulking compound and lye, or effectively gassed groundhogs that threaten the stability of house and barn foundations.

But it's not just critters that Trapper outwits; he even outsmarts vegetables, and predicts the weather through "Mother Nature".

Not only does he get rid of varmints, he gets rid of them in unusual and innovative ways, borne from a lifetime of knowledge gathering and experimentation. And he does it with such zest and garrulous nature that he's an instant hit wherever he goes.

He is not an exterminator. He is licensed by the State of Ohio as a "Wildlife Nuisance Trapper". He makes his own traps and delights in finding inexpensive, nontoxic solutions to the most common household pest problems.

Many of his tools and techniques are entirely original. He says, "It doesn't come from books, it comes from actually doing things".

Catching the animals alive without harming them, he takes them back to his little menagerie on his own property, feeds and observes them for a few days, and releases them into heavily wooded areas or park reserves. He cautions all never to touch or handle the animals directly.

Mr. Bailey worked for the Youngstown Sheet & Tube Company 30 years, retiring in 1977. He also operated a farm and trucked numerous livestock and performed veterinary work. To say he is retired is a misnomer. In his trappings alone, he has driven thousands of miles, as he covers area counties.

Not only does he help out with 4–H projects, senior citizen groups, and many organizations, he books scores of speaking engagements. And his flair and style of presentation, coupled with his contagious laughter, truly captures his audience. He also appears on television for informative segments as "The Friendly Trapper". He is a walking resource of helpful information on just about any pest related problem.

PESTS & INSECTS IN YOUR HOME

ANTS

There are ant problems all over the country. No matter what state I get my mail from there seems to be an ant problem. Also, when I get on radio that goes into 4, 5, or 30 states at one time – like the other night when I was on a radio program that went into 30 some states – I heard about ant problems. Okay, the carpenter ant is active and it's chewing and making sawdust. I'm using something that is so simple to get the job done. I want you to use 20 Mule Team Borax freshener. It's in a green box, and there's 20 teams of mules behind the little girl that's on the picture holding a whip. Sprinkle the 20 Mule Team Borax where the ants are traveling. I guarantee they'll be belly up in the morning! That's the end of them. Now also if the humidity is very high the soap can crystallize. You'll have to do it again. And it won't be long that you can put your mind at ease because you unloaded a problem putting down the ants.

Go down in the cellar if you have one and throw some of that mixture up by the water pipes. Those ants come in, in a crack somewhere in the cellar and come up the cold water pipes, up the electric wires, up the gas line. This way they'll get to feeding on it down in the cellar and chances are they aren't even going to make it upstairs. It's getting the job done. It's doing a beautiful job.

You can also use Diazinon in your cellar; however, open your cellar windows to allow the odor to escape. Spray between the beams, water pipes, dryer plug, and electric stove. When finished spraying your basement, close the cellar door, and place a rug under the bottom of the door so the odor does not permeate the upstairs.

If you notice a saw dust trail, you have carpenter ants – the large black ants, which will infest your home if left unattended.

RECIPE FOR INDOOR ANTS

1 Tbsp. boric acid, 1 Tbsp. alum (these products can be purchased in a drugstore), 1 Tbsp. sugar, and 1 Tbsp. flour. Mix all ingredients together and place in the areas where the ants are travelling. For example, under the kitchen sink, behind the stove, refrigerator, etc.

BATS

A bat can enter your home through a hole or crack the thickness of a yardstick. They enter through the chimney, the pipe from your furnace and into your cellar, by maneuvering their bodies under the flashing of your roof, through shutters, or through the clothes dryer vent. When a bat does enter your house, it will leave its body odor, which will attract other bats, and they too will enter. In less than a week, you may have several bats in your home. Bats will come up from basements, usually under the cellar door, seeking the light which attracts insects on which they feed. If they do accumulate in your attic, for instance, the bat dirt throws off a gas that can kill a human.

Here's a way to help you keep the bats out of your house. So you turn around and you take a plastic bag and you go around the hole or crack. You fasten that with duct tape and you cut the bottom of the plastic bag off. You can sit out there at night and watch the bats come down that plastic bag and out in the atmosphere. They can't get back in. You keep the bat from getting back in your house and you save the bat. We need every bat we can get. One bat will catch like 300 mosquitos in an evening. You also are helping the environment.

One precaution would be to place a screen over your chimney; however, make sure the holes are large enough to let your chimney breathe, allowing the smoke to escape.

To chase bats out of your house or chimney, get a few coffee cans. Pour three inches of water into the can; place a sulfur candle in the center. The lit candle produces a sulfur odor which will chase the bats outside.

Or, take four to five small moth balls and place them in an onion sack or a nylon stocking, tie it shut, and place it behind the shutter; bats find this smell repulsive. They also hate a product called Bat and Squirrel Chase. It is very potent and will do the job.

Remember, if you ever see a bat, raccoon, skunk, or fox during the day time, these animals are very sick, and are most likely rabies carriers. Call the police or game protector for them to dispose of the rodent. If you are bitten, contact your physician immediately.

If a bat or bird enters your home or business, and the structure has high ceilings, you can use a glue board trap to catch him. Take a piece of wood 2" x 2", and place it perpendicular under the trap. To secure the wood to the trap, drive a roofing nail through the top of the trap into the 2" x 2" underneath. Be sure the 2" x 2" is long enough to reach the ceiling. When the bird or bat is flying in the area, push the glue board up and catch him. They cannot escape a good, tacky, glue board trap.

"TRAPPER BAT TALE"

I had a lady call me. She says, "Trapper, I hate to call you, it's 10:30 at night, but I live alone, about thirty five miles from you and I have a bat in my house." I said, "Oh! O.K., you have to listen to what I say. I want you to shut all the lights out – every light has to be out. Open up the front door and put a floor lamp out there. And the bat will go out 90 miles per hour. It's attracted to go towards the lights. That's why you see bats always flying around security lights." Well you know, she didn't listen to me. She didn't sit in the chair, she didn't sit in the couch. She went down to the cellar and pulled the main switch. Now she turned right around and went outside without a chair and held a flashlight. The bat came out so fast, it knocked her over. It didn't even take fifteen minutes. Just one other way of getting a bat out of your house.

CHIPMUNKS AND RED SQUIRRELS

If you hear nuts rolling or a chewing sound, most likely you have these critters in your attic. Cut up a few onions and place them in the area. Mothballs work also. Then, look for their entrance hole. Go into your attic on a sunny day, turn all the lights off; you should be able to spot the hole where they are getting in.

Also, check the flashing on your chimney; they could get under the flashing and into the attic. Repair the hole as soon as possible. Stuff it with steel wool in the meantime, as they cannot chew through this substance. To patch the hole, which can be as small as the diameter of a quarter or smaller, use screen. Do not use a board, as they can and will chew through it.

Now that you have found their entry, you have to catch them. Buy a Havahart trap; it can catch one squirrel at a time. The trick to using this trap is to glue the bait to the paddle. Most important – use dog or cat food for bait. Chipmunks like either. They also like walnuts, hickory nuts, butternuts, acorns, and beechnuts. Or, simply glue a peanut to the trap pedal and the door will slam as the little pest tries to loosen it.

"TRAPPER CHIPPIE STORIES"
Car Won't Start

One woman told Trapper that chipmunks got into her new Cadillac and chewed the insulation off all the electrical wiring under the dash and in the engine compartment – from headlights to taillights. Explain that to the insurance company!

The Mysterious Garage Door

Another woman called because her garage door was opening and closing "on it's own"! Chipmunks again. I got a phone call one day and the lady said, "Trapper, you have to get over here right away!" I said, what's the problem, ma'am? She replied, "My garage door keeps going up and down." I said, "I'm not an electrician." "Trapper, I know you can help me, I am 86 years of age and I don't know anyone else to call. I live on a highway, please come over." It was an easy house to find because the garage door was going up and down, up and down. I went into the garage, found the fuse box and backed out the fuse. And, what did I find wrong? Ha! A chipmunk got up there and chewed the insulation off the wires. The wires got together and shorted the wires and she had a problem. I repaired the wires and sealed off the area where the chipmunks were getting in and solved that one.

Chippie Inside

Yet another woman called mystified because "my dogs are going crazy, they're tearing pillows off the couch, and my son's boots are full of dog food!" "Chippies", the Trapper diagnosed.

FLEAS

Dogs have a problem – the fleas. There are many products on the market we can use to take care of them; one is rubbing alcohol.

Take your long or short hair dog outdoors or in the garage. Using rubbing alcohol, rub the dog the opposite way the fur is laying. Start at the tail and neck because the fleas may enter the dog's ear and make him extremely irritable. You can also use rubbing alcohol on a cat; take it outdoors and rub the same way.

Alcohol is inexpensive and economical, very effective, and will solve the flea problem.

For a rather large dog that lives outside, feed him a half a clove of garlic twice a month. You'll find the following to be evident every two weeks:

1. The dog will automatically be wormed.

2. The garlic odor will keep the fleas away form your dog; however, your dog will have "garlic breath.

Another item we can use is a fantastic product by Avon called SSS Skin So Soft, which is a bath oil. Once a week, take your dog outside and rub him with a piece of cotton doused with SSS. The fleas, gnats, or sower flies may fly around your dog, but they will not land on him. Also does the job on horses, cats, and cattle.

Yet another flea eliminator is a modified plastic vinegar jug. The holes should be the diameter of a quarter or golf ball. Now, mix some soapy, sudsy water, and place this solution in the bottom of the jug; place a white light inside. Set this flea trap close by where your dog or cat lies the most. The white light draws the fleas into the jug, the solution gets on their wings, and they can not escape the jug. By morning, you see the little specks of "pepper" in your trap.

Black walnut leaves inside or outside your home will get the job done too. They emit a pungent odor the fleas find repulsive. When the leaves begin to fall, rake up a bushel or so and store them. Use either brown or green leaves.

For outdoor dogs, place the leaves in the dog's box along with a couple of moth balls. For indoor dogs, lay a piece of plastic on the floor behind a couch or chair. Place paper over the plastic and put about a handful of the leaves on the paper. Black walnut leaves are free; you just have to find the tree and gather the leaves!

Or, try an aluminum pie pan, fill with soapy water in a pet area, and place a Christmas tree light or flashlight above it. The light's heat will fool the fleas into thinking they are jumping toward body warmth.

The gals do a great job vacuuming the carpet; they sweep and place the sweeper back into the closet. The swept up fleas will walk right back out again onto the carpet! To remove and keep fleas out of your carpet, do the following.

Move your furniture to one side of the room, and sprinkle table salt onto that area. The salt will burn the fleas on contact; they're dead. Use talcum powder, baby powder, and let it stand on the carpet for 30 – 40 minutes. Now, here's the trick. Place a couple of moth balls in the sweeper bag. Plug an extension cord onto the sweeper enabling you to take it outside. Vacuum the area very thoroughly; do not turn the sweeper off inside your home. Take it outside and turn it off. Now, start your sweeper outside, if fleas start coming out, the sweeper will suck them up again. While you are outside, change the bag. Repeat this process for the other side of the room.

20 Mule Team Borax freshener will kill fleas on your dog. Rub the dog and keep your dog dry. Rub it through the fur and the fleas will die. Then, comb the dog well and the fleas will be belly up.

FLY TRAP

LET'S MAKE A FLY TRAP

Let's make ourselves a fly trap. We're going to turn around and we're going to use a mayonnaise jar and I want to cut a piece of cardboard out that will fit the top of the jar. The diameter of that. And then you make 5 or 6 or 8 holes in that cardboard, the diameter of a lead pencil. Now let's take a banana skin and rub some sugar on it. Also, tie a piece of thread to that. Now we're almost ready to start to put this together. We're going to put some strawberry jelly on top of the cardboard. Now we're going to make real soapy water and fill the jar about half full. Let's turn around and lower the banana skin to the water putting the string on the outside. Now we're going to take the cardboard you've cut out and place the strawberry jelly towards the water. Now go around there with freezer tape or duct tape and you've got yourself one heck of a beautiful fly trap. Put it up in the attic – it doesn't cost anything – and you'll catch all your flies before they turn around and get into your house through the downstairs.

Another Fly Trap

Okay, now we're going to make another fly trap and what we're going to do is make this in a sponge cake pan. Why? Because it's plastic and you can see straight through it and it's a fun thing for the kids. Let's take a sponge cake pan, I don't care if it's the size of a basketball in diameter or a half moon where you have half a sponge cake. But I want it all to be plastic. Then, go to the bottom of the sponge cake pan and drill a hole about a half inch in diameter. Now we're going to take a screen and we're going to make a circle out of it and twist it so it looks like an ice cream cone. We're going to go over the hole and glue that to the sponge cake pan. Now take your scissors and snip off the top of that so the fly can come through the bottom of that and come straight up on through. Now just make it about the diameter of a lead pencil. Now we can use all kinds of meat that you would ordinarily throw away. How about a piece of liver? It doesn't matter, there's pork or veal. How about a piece of raw fish? How about a banana skin with sugar on it? Just lay it in the bottom of that sponge cake pan. Now, put the lid on it. Raise it off the ground. If you want to put 2 or 3 legs on it that's okay. You can use a 2" x 4" or a 1" x 4" or whatever you want to use or don't put any legs on it at all and get it off the ground by using a couple of bricks or 2" x 4" blocks.

What happens is that the fly will eventually go underneath that pan and through that funnel after that meat and won't know how to get out. I've seen them loaded already. Just loaded with the old fashioned flies.

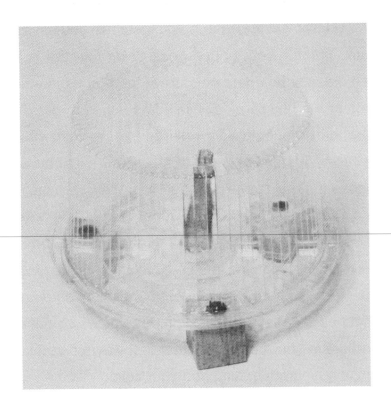

MICE AND RATS

Boil the mouse trap in an old coffee can; this will take away any body odor or other odor on the trap. Set the trap by using 1 tsp. peanut butter, 1 tsp. strawberry jelly, and 2 drops of cooking anise. Mix together and place on the paddle of the trap. This odor is unusual from all other odors and will attract the mice.

Mice will get into your house because you have a sump pump. The mouse goes down into the hole and digs the hole and gets down there and chews a hole in the plastic pipe. He'll find a way to get the pipe that's separated from tile to tile. You get yourself some aluminum gutter guard. Break off about 12 inches long, pull the plug out from the sump pump and stuff the pipe full of that gutter guard. The water is free to go. It takes care of all the snakes and all the mice from coming into your cellar. They go down the pipe, climb on the stem of your electric cord and climb up the slot that the sump pump comes out of and get in your cellar. Another fast way for keeping those guys from getting into your cellar.

"TRAPPER RAT TALE"

One day I got called up by Youngstown State University because a sewer rat came up through the commode and I have never seen that happen before. When I got the phone call, I went down there immediately. And I set my traps on the floor and all the office employees went home. Well, in the morning, I caught the rat. There's a little flap inside the commode and sometimes the rat will get it's nose in there and come up into the commode. So I climbed on the radio and I told the story and I said "For Heavens sake, always look before you sit down!"

MOTHS

You know as you watch your television sometimes you're going to see a little moth flying around. Now that's not the moth that's going to eat your material. This is called the old pantry moth. And sometimes it's called the drug store beetle. And that guy's going to lay all kinds of larva around. And on that larva you're going to get little black insects. Now those black insects are going to get into your spaghetti, macaroni, and into your breakfast cereal. They are so strong – those little guys – they will chew straight through plastic. Nothing holds them out except glass and a metal lid. If you have a plastic lid on a jar, they'll chew through the plastic lid to get inside. How do you solve that problem? Well number one, to catch the moth they make moth traps. Hardware stores have a nice moth trap. It's very easy to put together. It's just cardboard. Moths are attracted to the odor and go in and get stuck. Now when you come to this other insect – what you do... you clean all your shelves out. Any dog food, cat food, or anything like that you want to save, put it in the freezer and shut the lid for a couple days. That way it's going to kill the larva and the eggs in there. Once you get the shelves all cleared off, use the 20 Mule Team Borax soap and put that all over your shelves. Now what takes place there, they're going to be belly up. Put that 20 Mule Team Borax on your shelves, between your storm windows if you have them. They'll be belly up.

Now there's no insect out there that can handle Teaberry gum. Teaberry gum still can be found. It's a great, great gum. I use it very often. Now put two sticks of Teaberry gum on every shelf you have. Regardless if you have a bad little insect or not. Sometimes those guys will get into your dried flowers. They'll thrive on that. And then the first thing you know your house is polluted. And you'll wonder where they came from. Well chances are you brought them home in cat food, or dog food, or in packages. You should turn around and put that into a freezer and shut the lid. Sometimes it takes 4 or 5 days to unload that larva and those eggs that get inside. But if you don't do that you'll have those little black insects all over the place. And they're going to be about the size of the head of a pin. That's how small they are.

They're even hard to catch with the naked eye. You'll also find the weevil in there. Another trouble maker. He's into your flour and he's into your sugar. Use the same method. Put the flour and sugar in your refrigerator when you bring it home or turn around and put it in your freezer and you won't have this problem.

RACCOONS

These animals are difficult to handle and can be very destructive to your property. They love the dark, sewers, and chimneys. Raccoons breed in the Spring; 63 days later there will be one to eight babies per mother wherever they have made their home.

The simplest entry into your house by a raccoon is through the chimney. Always have a guard or screen over the chimney. Trapper has designed a trap that fits over the top of the chimney. Trapper would first lower a coffee can with a smoke bomb inside down into the chimney with a rope. Then he would place his home–made trap over the top of the chimney. When the smoke bomb ignites, the smoke will drive the adult raccoons up into the trap. Next, he would go inside to the fireplace, open the damper, and remove the little ones. Sometimes, baby raccoons will come right to him. Also helpful is a mirror and flashlight to see just where the critters are nestled. If a raccoon can maneuver his head into a hole, be certain he will be able to get his body inside too!

Now in a town that chimney represents a den tree. That raccoon will go right up that downspout. Guaranteed – right up the downspout. And down the chimney head first. And she'll go down there and have her babies. And you had better have your damper closed. And you'd better have glass doors in

front of your fireplace. Now what's going to take place is that she's going to have her little ones. Now we've got another problem. Why do you have a problem? Because you don't have no chimney guard on. You've got to have a chimney guard on. And what you're doing – the raccoon and other things are going to go down your chimney. Everything is going to stay down there. All the birds, all the squirrels are going to stay down there. Then you'll have to get someone with a license to take that raccoon out of there. And he'll have to have a trapper's nuisance license. That's the way it is in the state of Ohio. And he'll come there and get that raccoon out of that chimney if he knows what he's doing.

Now sometimes the gas fumes will come up and put the birds to sleep or squirrel to sleep and down in the chimney they'll fall. Or, the first thing you know you'll hear something running down in your cellar. And that's how that all happened because you had no chimney guard. Now let me tell you something, if you have a chimney guard on there you'd keep everything out.

"TRAPPER RACCOON TALES"
Into Cookie Jars Too!

A man called Trapper stating he had a raccoon in his kitchen sink eating cookies! Sure enough, when Trapper arrived, the raccoon was doing just that. The varmint had entered through the pet flap in the door and raided the cookie jar!

Sitting on a Raccoon

Here's another true story that you think would never happen to you. Got a call from a lady and she said, "Trapper, hurry over immediately, I'm sitting on a raccoon." I said, "No way can you be sitting on a raccoon, they'll tear you apart." "It's the truth, I'm in my 80's and please come over." My wife and I jumped into the truck and when we got there, this is exactly what happened. The raccoon had climbed a tree, walked across a limb and got into a bedroom and started down the steps. At the very bottom of the steps, the lady saw the raccoon and shook a newspaper. The raccoon ran and jumped into the clothes hamper. And, when I got there and knocked on the door the lady was waving her hands for me to come on in. "Hurry, I'm sitting on this raccoon!"

Well, she was right, it was the first time I ever saw anyone sitting on a wild animal...sort of.

I took that clothes hamper outside and snared the raccoon. I do guarantee you one thing, those clothes will never go back into a closet again. The clothes were all torn to shreds. The break that happened to that lady is that the phone was near her hamper.

Now He Needs to Use the Bathroom!

A raccoon had entered a home through the chimney and proceeded into the bathroom. The door was closed. The critter broke both toilet seats, knocked down the towel rack, cracked the window, and gnawed a hole at the base of the floor, crawled up inside the wall and fell sound asleep. Trapper shined a mirror and flashlight on him and the raccoon never budged. So, Trapper put a cage with bait in the bathroom. The raccoon came out sometime during the night, went into the trap, ate the lure, realized he was trapped, so decided to tear the linoleum off the floor!

The Furnace Room Varmint

A terrified woman called Trapper during the wee hours of the morning stating there was some kind of animal in her furnace room. She was alone and frightened and asked if he could come right away. Trapper asked her what kind of noises the critter was making. She said the sounds were horrible screeching noises. Trapper told her to place a blanket at the bottom of the door and go to bed, and he would be out first thing in the morning. At 7:00 a.m. sharp the woman rang his phone again, and Trapper was on his way with full gear, tennis racquet, badminton racquet, and even his gun. The woman greeted him anxiously and still petrified, rattling on about the creature. Trapper asked her to "Shhh", as he placed his fingers over his lips. Trapper kept hearing little squeak sounds. He figured there were four ways to get into the furnace room, and there was a closet adjacent to the room. Maybe the critter was in the closet. As he slowly opened the closet door with gun in hand — what do you think he found? Her smoke detector warning her that the batteries are weak!

Little Devils

I tell you, if you're in an area where there are raccoons, read this carefully. A local doctor had just purchased a new automobile and he took the children to the ice cream store to get a little treat. When he left home, he left his three car garage wide open. He pulled his new car in and left the windows down. Little did he know, three raccoons had gotten in the garage while he was gone. He went to bed, got up in the morning and went to the garage. Those raccoons had torn up the inside of the car like you would never believe. The upholstery was shredded and I got the phone call to come and try to get the raccoons. I captured two quickly and set the trap to catch the last one alive also. I used two white marshmallows and had him park his car outside and we caught the other raccoon that night.

ROACHES

ROACH RECIPE

Take one cup of flour, one small onion chopped, 16 oz. boric acid powder, and 1/4 cup vegetable oil. Add just enough water to form a stiff dough. Shape into balls the size of marbles. Place the balls where roaches are hiding and/or travelling.

ROACH TRAP

Into a glass put 2–3 Tbsp. of bacon grease. Place a chunk of banana, about two inches high in the center of the glass. Take your finger and make a ring inside the glass by using Vaseline one–half inch from the top of the glass.

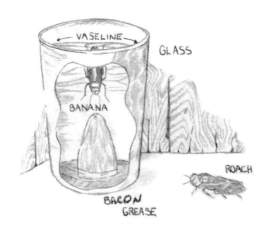

Place in the area where the roaches are travelling. They will smell the banana, go through the Vaseline into the bacon grease and cannot escape. Several roaches can be caught in one glass. Of course, you would "pitch" the roach filled glass!

Or, place strips of duct tape, sticky side up, with pieces of banana on it where the roaches travel. They will be unable to escape once they get onto the tape.

The other thing I want to talk about is you can use the 20 Mule Team Borax freshener and turn around and go down to the store and purchase yourself some coconut flakes or just all chopped up coconut. You use equal parts of Borax and coconut (very important). Mix this up, keep it dry, and put it where your roaches are and I guarantee you in another day or so they'll be belly up.

Well if you have a terrible roach problem, there's a number of ways to solve it. And there's absolutely no roach out there that can handle cedar wood oil. Now where do you get cedar wood oil? At the lumber company! That's the only place I was ever able to find that product. When you get the cedar wood oil, you go down to the cellar and you paint your pipes with that. Paint the corners of your home with that. Put it on the top plate. That will discourage them from coming upstairs. Once they start multiplying on you, you're in big trouble.

SPIDERS

The Hedgeapple tree, plentiful in the Ohio area, is also called a "Monkey Ball", but the correct name is Osage Orange. The tree is very green and can grow as high as 50 feet with a diameter of a bushel basket. A squirrel would not attempt to run up the trunk, as it is extremely thorny.

In the Fall, after the first severe frost, the fruit will drop to the ground. They will be about the diameter of a grapefruit. Be sure to select the fruits that have fallen by mother nature after the frost, as opposed to the fruits that fall as a result of harsh winds, which will force them down. If they drop prematurely, they will be soft, and will not hold up. If you select the Fall fruits, they will keep all through the winter and last until the last week of May. They will turn yellow and black, and even into a brown color. Collect bushels of them if you can, and share them with your friends and neighbors. People in the South are especially fond of them.

To rid your house of spiders or roaches, place four or five of these fruits in your cellar, one underneath your kitchen sink, and perhaps one under the bathroom sink.

The fruit throws off an odor repugnant to the insects, not killing them, but rather forcing them outside.

Florists also use them in floral arrangements and they make great Christmas gifts.

If you are lucky enough to find an Osage Orange tree, you have a gold mine.

SQUIRRELS

If the fox squirrel is down in your fireplace chimney you don't have to kill or hurt it. Just get yourself a fat rope, put it down the chimney because he can't get out of there unless he has something to climb. So use a nice long thick rope, big in diameter and tie it to the chimney. Or in my case I use two 2" x 2"s. I put one 2" x 2" down into the chimney, then the next one I put right along side of it and duct tape it so that it goes clear down to the bottom of the fireplace and hits the damper. That squirrel is so happy to get out of there. He knew he made a mistake. He'll climb up the 2" x 2" and turn around and he's out in the wild. It didn't take long to solve that problem. You didn't hurt the animal. You don't need a professional to get that job done.

Now listen to what I'm saying and pay attention. The red squirrel (also called the pine squirrel) and a chipmunk and a flying squirrel are deadly on your electric wires when they get inside your home. They're going to get inside your home and they're going to tear the insulation up like you'd never believe. What you do, you get a live trap. And you put it inside the attic. Then you turn around and you glue the peanuts to the paddle. I love to use the peanuts in the shell. Then if the live trap has two ends you put some peanuts on the floor – one or two that's all. And break one of them in two so they get the message and smell. They'll go in there and they think they can get in there and back out. Now that's not going to happen. Because you glued the peanuts to the paddle. A little peanut butter on top of that won't hurt anything. Just a touch of it. And you caught yourself the squirrel – the little trouble maker.

Now how in the world did that squirrel get in there? Well you know we have beautiful roof vents. Fifty dollars and on up in price. They give you a 10 cent screen. You heard me a 10 cent screen. Those squirrels will go underneath that roof vent and smash it down. And then he's inside your attic. In the winter time it's the easiest way to track a squirrel because of the snow on your roof. When there's snow on the roof you know exactly where they're going in and going out. Another bad spot on the house is the little roofing by the rain spouting. The pine squirrel, the red squirrel sit in that rain spouting and they sit there and chew and chew and chew until he's inside your home. That's how he gets in there. Now if that happens to you all you do is take a piece of aluminum, go behind the rain spouting and block the hole up after you catch him. You can solve this problem. You spent about 25 cents plus the cost of the trap. There's all kinds of traps out there. Make sure that the man that sells you a trap has used one himself, or has the experience where he sold traps to get the job done. It doesn't take a big trap. It takes a little trap. Then where the mechanism is on the trap, you turn around and you use just a little bit of bacon grease to lubricate that paddle or WD 40. You spray that in there. And they're going to go in there and get back out. But if you've got the peanuts on the paddle they can't go anywhere.

YARD AND GARDEN VARMINTS

REMEMBER...

If you ever see a bat, raccoon, skunk, or fox during the day time, these animals are very sick, and are most likely rabies carriers. Call the police or game protector for them to dispose of the rodent. If you are bitten, contact your physician **immediately!**

ANTS

Ants are everywhere. Ortho has a great liquid product called Diazinon. Dilute 3/4 cup to one gallon of water. Twice a year, Spring and Fall, spray just above the grass, around the bushes, on the sides of your home or building, porch, sidewalk, etc. The solution will penetrate into the soil, killing all kinds of ants, centipedes, grasshoppers, ladybugs, and measuring worms. Rain will not dilute this solution, as it is very potent.

I am a great believer in putting detergent soap outside. I like it. It rolls over the water bugs, and a lot of insects. Also, use Tide outside on an anthill or 20 Mule Team Borax, it will also kill your ants outside. Now it may burn your grass. But where you have an ant hill you don't have any grass growing anyhow. Isn't that economical! Now when the dew comes or when it rains that's going to go down inside there and it's going to do the ants in regardless of what kind they are. I think that's a nice way to unload an ant problem. I'm a great believer in using diazinon. I make it very strong, very strong, and I spray that above the grass but against the side of your home. You put all your windows down. Yes, it is toxic, but on the other hand it's all going to disappear in 2 or 3 hours. What will it do for you? Well there's not too many insects out there — red ant or the black ant — that can handle diazinon. If you can do that around your house once a month you can save a big problem. What you're going to do is your going to save yourself some money and get the job done and 8 ounces is all you're going to have to buy to solve that problem.

You can turn around also on an ant problem and you go and get yourself some boric acid. It's economical, you only need 4oz. And then you turn around and use equal parts of boric acid with a nice mint flavored apple jelly. What we're going to do there is by using equal parts – you put this on a piece of cardboard - the apple jelly draws their attention and the boric acid will put them down. This is another way to unload an ant problem.

THE GREAT OUTDOORS

You know you have a tremendous problem with ants when you're having a picnic. Now this is what you do. You have 4 or 5 or 6 legs on a picnic table. Then you want to find a pie pan or you turn around and use jar lids depending on the diameter of the legs on your table. You go underneath the leg and set that leg into the pie pan or jar lid. Then you put vegetable oil there. Now you do that to all the legs and there's no ant gonna crawl up the leg of the table to get at your cake. No ant's going to eat my cake – I'll guarantee you that! Now if you're underneath a tree there's always the possibility of an ant falling down on your table. So if you want to control the ants on a beautiful day with a picnic just follow those instructions and you won't have ants eating your cake.

BAT TRAPS

To catch a bat, get a five gallon bucket, used motor oil, and a piece of flexible hose about the diameter of a tennis ball. Pour four quarts of oil in the bucket. Hang the bucket onto your house with a rope or wire. Connect the hose into the hole; the bat will crawl into the hose and fall into the oil. With the oil on his wings, he'll be immobile. You can then place a screen over the top of the bucket, allowing other birds to escape the punishment and bury the entire bucket.

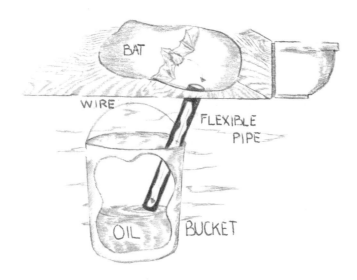

You can also catch a bat in a dip net or stun him with a tennis or badminton racquet. When he's down, throw a coat or blanket over the rodent and dispose of him.

Always wear long heavy gloves to protect your hands from a possible bite, as bats are rabies carriers.

Yet another bat trap is to get some hardware cloth (screen – it comes 24" high), the center of an angel food cake pan, and a 6" diameter plastic butter container. Wire the screen onto the outside base of the cake pan forming a tube like structure. At the top opening, place the butter container right side up, and secure with wire to the screen. Make a handle with wire and place in the center of the trap. This will enable you to fasten the trap to the wall. Now, connect the trap to the outside of the building at the hole, flush against the wall. The bats will come out of the house through the hole in the wall, then through the cake pan hole, and into the trap.

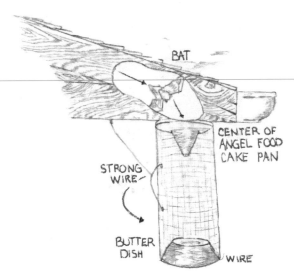

BAT

CENTER OF ANGEL FOOD CAKE PAN

STRONG WIRE

BUTTER DISH

WIRE

BEAVERS

A "FOOLPROOF WAY" TO GET RID OF BEAVERS

To unload a beaver problem, take a PVC pipe and cut it into two five foot lengths. Then use a 45 degree elbow and connect the five foot pieces. Now, dig down in the dam and put the pipe into the dam. The next day it will be covered with sticks and mud. We've now dropped the water from four to eight feet.

Take the pipe out and lower it one more time. Block the pipe very good with rods or thick twigs. The beaver will hit the road! He just cannot figure out why his dam is leaking water. They want an area that is high and dry. Then you will find the dens where the beavers are living. There's also a live beaver trap that you can use and then relocate the beaver.

P.S. Put plugs in each end of the pipe so the beaver cannot plug up the holes!

BEES

There are two ways to catch bees that are bothering you in your picnic area. Take pie pans and put them on the ground. In some pans pour a little honey, enough to coat the bottom. Also, in the other pie pans use orange juice. The bees will either get stuck in the honey or the orange juice will ferment in the sun and the bees will drink the juice and drown. You shouldn't get stung and they shouldn't bother you.

To kill ground bees or yellow jackets, go outside at 10:00 pm (at night) and pour scalding hot water into the hole. You can also use Sevin (50%). It is white like flour and can be bought at a hardware store. Pour the Sevin down into the hole. Problem solved.

BIRDS

Well lots of people have problems with birds in their shanties or maybe the woodpecker's pecking your house. Well you know most people can get themselves a black plastic bag, and you turn around and you cut some strips about one inch wide. And you staple that or duct tape it to some twine or string or rope. And you hang that where the woodpecker is bothering you. And the first thing you know, you've stopped that woodpecker from bothering your house.

Another thing you can do is you can hang balloons in that area to stop them.

Now in a shanty or in a garage, you hang those black plastic strips down. And the wind will blow that and the birds are afraid of black.

Now you can do the same thing over your garden. You don't have to have the birds eating your seeds after you've planted your garden. You turn around and you make an X. And then you tie the black ribbon there and make sure that the wind can move it. And you're going to find out that it won't be long that those birds are gonna fly because they just cannot handle black plastic. Something simple, something easy, and every-body has black plastic.

When you go past a used car lot they have all those colors up there on top of the cars and rope hanging down. That's not so much to catch our attention. That's to keep the birds from white washing their cars. That's what that's all about.

Birds also like to make nests in the center of your outside hanging flower baskets. To discourage them from doing this just put some of your old pencils (point side up) into the center of the basket. Birds can't sit on anything sharp...Problem solved!

BOX TRAPS

LIST OF MATERIALS

Item	Quantity	Size				Type
Door	1	¾" x	7¼"	x	8½"	white pine no. 2
Rear Partition	1	¾" x	7½"	x	8½"	white pine no. 2
Top and Bottom	2	¾" x	9"	x	24"	white pine no. 2
Sides	2	¾" x	8½"	x	24"	white pine no. 2
Treadle	1	¾" x	7¼"	x	11"	white pine no. 2
Galvanized Tin (for door)	1		7¼"	x	5½"	28 gauge
Hardware Cloth	1		7½"	x	8½"	¼" hardware mesh
Trip Wire	1				15"	no. 9 gauge hard galv.
Fulcrum Wire	1				10"	no. 8 gauge hard galv.
Door Hinge Wire	1				10"	no. 9 gauge hard galv.
Screw Eyes	4	No. 112				
Staples (for door and hardware cloth)	14	No. 14			¾"	
Nails (for tin)	10				½"	
Box Nail (for bait)	1	8d				
Box Nails	16	6d				
Wood Screws, Flat Head	10				1½"	
Wood Screws, Rd. Hd. (for door and fulcrum)	2				1"	

Side View, Trap Set

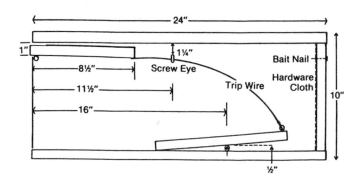

CANADIAN HONKERS

Let's talk a little bit about the Canadian Honker. I'm getting a lot of calls on the Canadian geese going on the grass and making a mess. In some cases it's so bad you can't walk without the droppings getting all over the soles of your shoes. It is so simple to control these guys. All I want you to do is turn around and get some paper, silver on one side and red on the other. It's kind of like a plastic paper that will stand the weather. Then you stretch this out. How do you do this? First I want you to take the paper about 12 inches long at least and stretch a line, a clothesline or something, around your property and every so often, every 3 feet, turn around and tie this red and silver paper on this line and let it hang down. Let it hang down like clothes on a clothesline. The Canadian Honkers cannot figure this out and they'll come up and go the other way. I've never yet had a Canadian Honker go underneath the red and silver paper. The last experiment I worked with I left an opening about 5 feet with no paper where on the other side the man is out there feeding ducks. He's feeding ducks in that opening and the Canadian Honkers are actually afraid to get on the grass. I've done one side of this man's property and what do you think happened? I chase all the Canadian Honkers on the other side of the lake and I had to go do that one. How do you get this paper? Call Agland Co–Op Inc. in Canfield, Ohio at (216) 533–5551 or 1–800–772–7707. Ask for the front desk and ask them for a roll of this red and silver paper. You get 250 feet and so you're going to be able to do your back yard and you're going to be able to keep your Canadian Honkers from getting on your grass. You don't have to put up with that. I probably could even do this across the lake and they wouldn't go underneath it. I haven't tried that yet but someday I will. Red and silver paper and you'll get that job done, I'll promise you that.

CATS

For problems with cats in your yard get some Lemon Grass Oil from a drug store. Soak some twine in it and then hang it up like a clothesline around your problem area.

Another way to solve this problem is to take a pie pan and melt some Vick's Vapor Rub or BenGay in it. Cats can not handle the odor of these. Again run twine or string through it and hang it up like a clothesline. Put the string or twine where the cats are bothering you.

Sometimes you like to catch a cat for one reason or another. And a lot of people can never catch a cat because they don't know how to handle it. What you do is try to get the rugs or rags or straw or grass or what ever the cat is lying on and you put it in your wire cage. Now, once you get this in the cage, the odor is there. Use some sardines or cat food and put a little bit on the outside of the cage and on the ground or the floor. The first thing you know, the cat will smell it's own body odor and go inside and then it is caught and caught live. Then you can take the cat to the veterinarian and he can turn around and do what ever you want done to the cat.

REMEMBER...

Neuter all your animals and we won't have all those little ones being produced.

CHIPMUNKS

You can make a trap from a scrub bucket. Place the bucket into the ground, exposing the mouth. Fill the bucket half way with water. Place a few peanuts in the shell that will float on the water. The chipmunk will jump into the bucket to get the food and will not be able to escape.

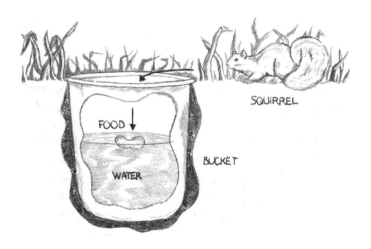

A chipmunk or red squirrel will chew insulation off your wiring. Take cheesecloth and cut little circles out about the diameter of a lead pencil. Roll the circles into tiny balls, moisten well with cooking oil, and place them into a jar lid. Place the lids outside under a board or tile where they will not be exposed to the weather. The animals will be attracted to this, eat it, and will destroy their digestive tract.

CAUTION...

Chipmunks are capable of collapsing a stone wall; attend to them immediately.

CATCHING CHIPMUNKS

There's another way to make a nice trap to catch the chipmunk alive. Get a pipe that is plastic and white, a PCP pipe about 20 inches in length. On the bottom of the pipe, use screen door screening and double it and place it over the end of the pipe. Use a radiator clamp or just use a wire and make a peanut butter ball about the size of a golf ball. Then, roll it down inside the pipe. Stand the pipe up off the ground and tie it to a post or tree around your garden. Put it off the ground about two inches so a mouse or chipmunk will smell it. They will go up the post and down inside that pipe and cannot get out. You can relocate that fellow if you want or take him down to the woods by putting a rag or rug over the end of it. The good Lord put all of this stuff on this earth for a reason. Only we have to get to the point where we have to protect our house and home. The chippie is deadly on your electric wires. He doesn't care what color they are. Lots of times I get all kinds of calls from people whose burglar alarms were set off by the chipmunk. Or they are in someone's automobile, or they chewed the wires on someone's tractor or combine or other equipment. One thing is for sure, the kitty cats will help you solve that problem. Guaranteed.

DEER

Get a bag of human hair clippings from the barber or hairdresser. Cut the bottom of a plastic jug. Using tape, make an "X" across the cut out bottom. Insert the hair; the hair will stick to the tape. Hang the jug upright near the garden or fruit trees. The jug will keep the hair dry, and the human scent will keep the deer away.

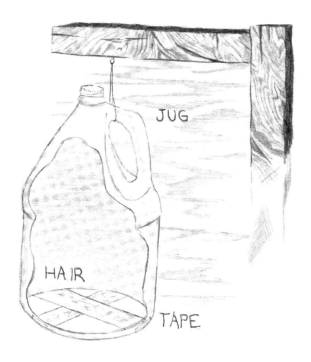

To keep deer out of your cornfield, use an electric fence that a farmer would use for cattle. Go nose high, then take a piece of metal and shape it like an apple. Paint it an apple red color and go to your local drug store and buy a pint of apple scent. Put it in a spray bottle and spray the painted apple. Deer will come up and lick it. All you'll see is white tail.

DEER WHISTLES

I have a lot of faith in deer whistles. They've saved my truck or my car five times. Now, there's all kind of deer whistles out there, but I like the ones that are in my book because they seem to get the job done. One whistle is for dogs, and the other is for deer. Well, not too long ago a deer jumped off the bank and went through the windshield and went straight back into the car. Now, you know that was very, very, very dangerous. The hooves are so sharp that they will just open you up. Both of the people, the man in the back seat and the woman in the front seat, got out without being injured. They were so fortunate. The hard part was trying to get the deer out of the car. They finally succeeded. How lucky they were— the good Lord was just on their side.

Another time, not too long ago, a lady was walking her dog as I approached and the dog took her into the ditch. He heard the whistles and they do work!

GARDENS

START A GARDEN

First, you must test the soil. Take a pipe about six inches long, any diameter, and push it into the soil in five places; one in each corner and one in the center. Mix all five soils and have it tested.

To save time by not planting seeds that will not grow in your garden, take a sponge with holes in it. Write the words cabbage, lettuce, beets, etc. or whatever you'll be planting on pieces of paper attached to toothpicks. Dampen the sponge and place two or three marked seeds inside. Set this on a piece of aluminum foil and place on top of the refrigerator. If the seeds do not germinate in the sponge, they will not germinate at all in your garden.

Soak some beans overnight and place between paper towels. If they sprout between the towels, they will sprout in your garden. If they don't, the seeds may be too old.

Fertilize your garden with human hair clippings. The nitrogen from the hair is great for your veggies. Use it when planting your veggies also. Dig a hole, scatter some hair clippings in the hole, then place your plant on top of the hair and cover with soil.

INSECT FREE GARDEN

No poison is necessary. After cabbage starts to grow, you will see a white butterfly land on the plants and lay eggs. The eggs will hatch into an insect, and the insect will chew holes in the cabbage. Make a solution of 3/4 cup table salt to one gallon of water. Pour a teacup of this onto the developing heads twice a week. The insects will die. This solution is also effective on small green worms that get into your cabbage. The cabbages will grow so hard and solid, they could be used as "bowling balls!" Their flavor will be enhanced from the salt solution. Great solution for broccoli and cauliflower too.

In a blender, mix one cup of garlic tops or two cloves of garlic, two Tbsp. of liquid dish washing soap, one tsp. of hot pepper seeds, and one cup of lime. Start the blender. Place the solution into a gallon bucket and mix with one gallon water. Spray your plants with the solution twice a week, (the soap will help hold the solution onto the plants).

CUCUMBERS IN A BOTTLES

Plant your cucumbers on the longest day of the year, June 21st. With a shotgun, make many holes in an old bucket. Fill the bucket with manure. Dig a hole and place the bucket inside the ground. Cover with dirt and place lime all around the area as far as you think the cukes will vine. Plant the cucumbers on the outside of the bucket. After they start to grow, take a bucket full of water and dump it in the bucket onto the manure. All of the roots will go toward the bucket and grow like mad. As the cukes vine, the bees will pollinate flowers, the flowers will turn into a cucumber. When the cukes reach the size of a lead pencil, place one into an empty ketchup bottle. Now, it will grow fast. When the sun hits the bottle, it will produce heat. Move the bottle close to the end of the stock. In no time, the cucumber will be fully grown inside the ketchup bottle. Break it from the vine, fill the bottle with cider vinegar and put the cap back on the bottle. Children as well as adults are amazed to see these "non–edible cukes."

Another cucumber trick is to plant cucumbers around a tree or lamp post. Dig a hole, put some manure in, then the cuke seeds. Run chicken wire up the tree and the vines up the wire. Very soon, you will have many cucumbers, and you won't have to bend down to pick them!

CAUTION...

Never pick cukes or beans when there is dew on the ground; you will blight them.

PEPPER PLANTS

Dig a hole. Tear the cardboard off a pack of matches; rip half of the matches off and throw them into the hole and spread around. Place dirt on top. Set the pepper plant on top of the dirt into the hole. Once the plant starts to grow, the roots will seek out the sulfur in the matches.

In the Fall, before the frost, select you best pepper

plant. Dig it up and place in a five gallon bucket with stones at the bottom. Put dirt all around the plant. Take it into your house and place by a well lit window. You can still enjoy peppers off the plant at Christmas time.

To grow peppers so big you would need a pound of hamburger to stuff them, put two tsp. of Epsom salts in one quart of water and fill spray bottles with the solution. Spray the bottoms of the plants twice a week. The results are nice large, flavorful peppers.

TOMATO PLANTS

Use fertilizer stakes "5–25–10". Simply place the stakes between the tomato plants. Also good for many other types of vegetables. As it rains and the dew falls, the gas is released to the roots as the veggies need it.

There is a tomato called "Keeper Tomato". This tomato will stay through the winter. Pick them, wrap them in newspaper and store in a cellar that is not heated; they will not rot.

To ripen tomatoes, put five into a brown paper bag when they are green. Add three apples and close the bag tightly. The gas from the apples will ripen the tomatoes. In seven days, you'll have red ripe tomatoes. And, if you place the bag in the sun, you'll have red tomatoes in four days.

WORMS IN YOUR GARDEN

Pick up worms whenever you see them and put them into your garden. They make holes in the soil to get air. When it rains, the holes fill up with water, and your garden will be able to breathe and be irrigated at the same time.

GROUNDHOGS

To spot a groundhog hole, look for the old fashioned large green horseflies scurrying above. These animals dig two holes to come and go. Purchase a gas cartridge which is 3 1/2 inches long and the diameter of a golf ball. Poke all the holes out as indicated and place the wick inside. Then, fill one hole with dirt from a five gallon bucket; light the wick, and throw the cartridge into the other hole. When it fires, fill that hole with dirt. The groundhogs will be "sound asleep" in about ten minutes. These creatures will do extensive damage to your property if left unattended.

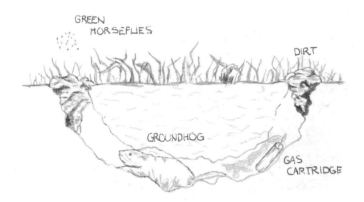

Take a rag soaked in gasoline. You're going to put the rag way back into the groundhog hole and then you're going to cover the hole up with dirt on top of the rag. It's not going to work! So, you're going to put a rock or something over the hole and you're going to put dirt around it and seal it tight. The groundhog has 2 holes so you've got to block up the other hole solid. That's one way. The other way is to get a paper bag that they have used to carry dog food in or farm feed for horse or cows and usually there's three bags in one. I run that all the way down into the soil clear up to my armpits than I put a pint of gasoline into the bag and roll the bag up and put a lot of dirt on top of the bag. Now what we've got to do is to seal that off. In both cases you turn around and you put dirt on top of it. If you want to you put some water on top of the hole, just a little bit, and put more dirt on top of it. The groundhogs cannot handle gas fumes. You'll put them to sleep right out in the center of your hay field or maybe into your fence row. Groundhogs are terrible on farm equipment and on livestock.

This takes care of a groundhog problem. You know the groundhog has usually two holes and sometimes they get carried away and they'll have 3 or 4 holes. Now the easiest way to do this is to turn around and fill all those holes up good and tight with dirt. Then you get yourself a plastic pipe or even a garden hose in some cases and you put that down into the last hole that's open (about 60 inches long). Now you pack dirt all around that plastic hose. Now this is very toxic – very toxic – so I put a funnel down into the garden hose or plastic hose. I use 3/4 cup of liquid bleach and one quart of clear ammonia. Now that's a terrible gas. Now once you do that you pull the hose out very, very slow. Then right away you keep on putting dirt on top of that hole you pulled the hose out of. And you'll put that guy to sleep and you spent about 59 cents to under a dollar. And that could be 3 or 4 groundhogs down there or maybe one groundhog down there and if they didn't dig back out you know you got the job done. And it's the easiest way for a farmer to get out there and tear around and get the groundhogs because if they dig a hole in the pasture or out in the field, first thing you know an animal is going to fall down – a horse, a cow, or what-ever and break a leg and now we've got another prob-lem. That will help to solve your groundhog problem like right now. Also, when you use the plastic pipe what I did is I turned around and took a broom handle and I put it inside and I sawed it off. Then I turned around and put a regular clamp around that broom handle, then I took an electric drill and drilled some holes at the end of the pipe. Now when you push the pipe down into the groundhog hole, it'll never plug up. Yet you put your solution down into the pipe by using that funnel and therefore you didn't waste it. You got the job done. You did not plug it up and you solved one heck of a big problem.

Another thing, when a groundhog is underneath a shanty or underneath a building, you block off all the holes going around. Use a 2" x 4" or 2" x 8" or some cement block and then you set a live trap right in front of that hole. Now apple is the best thing to use all year round. They love apple. They're a vegetarian. That's why you don't have a garden left. Then once you get that trap set then I block the sides off with pieces of cardboard. Now there's only one way for that ground-hog – that's out of the hole and straight in the trap and you caught that guy alive. Now you can do whatever you want to do with him.

JAPANESE BEETLES

JAPANESE BEETLE TRAP

Save a glass pint jar with a lid and a 2–liter plastic pop bottle. Make a hole in the lid of the jar the size of the pop bottle opening; put 2 Tbsp. of used motor oil in the jar. Cut out two 3" x 4" windows in the body of the pop bottle allowing the insects to enter.

Now make about three holes in the bottom of the bottle and run wires through enabling you to hang the trap from a tree or bush. Be sure your wires extend into the bottle also. Now turn the bottle upside down and hang a small metal can which has been cut in half onto the wires, creating a little "feeding cup." Place the opening of the bottle into the lid hole. Be sure this connection is very secure. Fill the feeder with fruit cocktail and hang the trap in the beetle area. The sun will ferment the fruit, it will attract the insects, they will get into it, get drunk, and fall into the oil.

Grubs come from Japanese beetles. In the Fall, the beetles will drop to the ground and bury themselves into the soil, then they are referred to as grubs. Eliminate them with Diazinon.

MICE AND RATS

Use a flat styrofoam tray. Mix one cup of portland cement and one cup of flour (both dry). The rodent will consume this mixture and plug up in three hours and die, (use cement without sand or gravel, we don't want to ruin his teeth!).

Also, take any jar lid and fill with dark carbonated cola. When the rodents drink it, their systems will plug up and, for example, expand a mouse's body to the size of a golf ball, and a rat's body to the size of a tennis ball. They cannot belch or regurgitate, and will literally blow up and die. Or, take a sponge and break it into pieces the size of a thimble and dip the pieces into bacon grease. This will destroy their digestive tract when eaten. And I guarantee you all four feet will be in the sky in the morning.

The glue boards used for bats and birds also do the job on the rats and mice. Place the traps where the rodents cross as they move from hiding places to feeding areas. Simply dispose of the board when the rodents enter.

Another method is to fill a scrub bucket half way with water and tie a stick to the handle, creating a ramp from the ground to the mouth of the bucket. Be sure the stick is firm and secure. Place a wire lengthwise through an empty baking soda can, allowing the can to spin freely. Secure each end of the wire to the mouth of the bucket. Coat the can with bacon grease, and generously sprinkle cookie, cake, or cracker crumbs onto it. The mice will crawl up the stick to get the crumbs, try to get onto the spinning can, and fall into the bucket for their last swim!

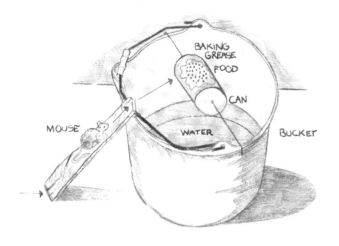

Also they love instant potato flakes, out of a box – that's right instant potato flakes.   Have a little jar lid with water on one side and a jar lid with instant potato flakes next to it. What they'll do is they eat that and they'll go get a drink of water. Now you see they can't vomit and they can't burp. The potato flakes will swell up in their body. And you solved that problem outside.

Now there's a very good product out there called Ro–dex. I mix the Ro–dex with peanut butter. Now that's farm seeds – oats, barley, rye – that's all in that Ro–dex. Now what are you doing? Well you're helping the farmers out. And if you put that in some tile, or in a plastic hose, or in a plastic pipe they'll go in there and eat that. Nothing else can get it. And the rat or the mouse will be belly up in the morning. It has strychnine in it and it's opened up to the public. Everything I talk about you can do because you can go into the store shelves and get it yourself.

You can also take a five gallon bucket or a 25 gallon barrel or a 50 gallon barrel. Now you run sticks up along side. We'll catch those rats and mice. Then you fill the container you are using half full of water. Then I go across that with some paper that you'd get from a pa-per bag that you'd get from a grocery store. And you stretch that over and you tie it with binder twine or duct tape and you make an X in the center of that bag, right on the top. That rat or mouse is going to go up that 2 x 4 or 2 x 2 or that stick and he's going to walk across to get that feed. Bird seed works well, hog feed, cow feed

– any kind of feed. Stick that on top and they'll walk across that and drop right down the bucket or in the pail, or in whatever you use up there. That works very, very good.

Now you people who are up in the mountains and have a cabin and you want to protect your place. Go get yourself some mouthwash bottles, the king size. A huh! Where do you get them? Recycling! They'll give them to you or maybe you'll have to pay a nickel for them. So what? It's the best mouse trap you can make. Now you take it up to the cabin and you stop and get yourself a gallon of this fluid that we put in the window washers in our cars. It won't freeze up. Just go half full and then anchor that bottle with some duct tape or a couple bricks and run a stick up there. From the ground up to the top. You want the hole the diameter of your big thumb. You're in tip top shape. Those mice will go down in there and they can't get out. They're attracted to the color. And the mouse loves to get into that solution. And he'll not get back out. I'll guarantee it!

Another way I'll do it. I'll take a 50 cup – 5 gallon – barrel if I got a bad rat problem. Then I'll go ahead and I'll get some binder twine or baler twine and I'll hang it up from the barn beam, almost to the barrel. I'll make a great big ball of peanut butter and stick it on to that binder twine. That rat will run up there and jump – just jump – at that peanut butter. He can't resist it. This is smelling good. This is a different odor than you have inside the barn. And the first thing you know he'll run and jump and fall in the barrel. You've got him trapped.

Now you folks have been running around and setting your mouse traps inside your home. There's nothing wrong with that. There's all kinds of mouse traps out there. Number one you made a mistake because you used butter or you used peanut butter. Erase that from your mind. They will lick it off and you'll not catch them. The first thing you do, you boil the traps in the water. I use a coffee can and then throw it away. That way you're taking all the body odor away from your traps. Then you turn around and you rub the base of the traps with bacon. Bacon that hasn't been fried. And you rub that on. They love to smell that. They'll go right to that. You can tie the bacon to the paddle. You also can use hard salami, cooked salami, pepperoni, ham rind, bacon rind. That's all going to work for you. And that way when it's tied to the paddle they can't get it.

Now you know if your bones aren't moving just right. You're kind of stoved up there. You know you can take a mouse trap and glue a nice dowel to it on the side. And you set the trap and you can always push it back under a chair or underneath your couch, or underneath a stand. That way you don't have to worry about getting down on your knees and can't get back up. You can sit in a chair for you older folks and you can solve that problem all by yourself. It works so nice and so easy. And you're going to be surprised how quickly you're going to catch the mouse.

MOLES

Wearing gloves, dilute one can of household lye with two gallons of water. Put this mixture into a sprinkling can, remove the head of the can, and pour into the mole holes. Moles will lick it and die. Or, shred bubble gum and place it down their holes. They'll never "blow bubbles" again!

Yet another effective way to rid your property of the pest is to tape a hose to the exhaust pipe of your garden tractor and run the hose into the hole. Start your tractor and let it run for 15 minutes. Moles as well as other rodents will die from the carbon monoxide. Have a wide shovel ready to strike them in case some moles escape the hole during this process.

Moles also like peanut butter. Set a mouse trap loaded with chunky peanut butter outside on the grass. Set a cardboard box with four holes the size of tennis balls over the trap. This will prevent cats and dogs from getting into the trap or carrying it off. Moles will enter through the holes, eat the peanut butter, and get caught in the trap.

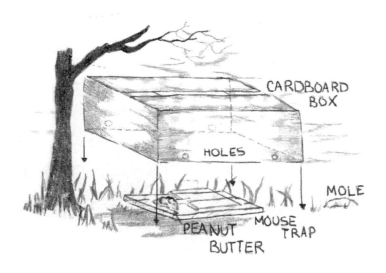

Also helpful is to spray your lawn with Ortho's Diazinon or similar insecticides to kill the beetle grubs in the soil on which the moles feed.

Are you having trouble with something eating your garden tomato or cucumber plant or even a squash plant of any kind? It could be a shrew, a ground mole, a squirrel or a rat or a mouse. Now how do you solve that problem? Well we have to protect our vegetables. It's no fun going out there and seeing that stuff destroyed. You find a product called Ro–dex and you take a ball of peanut butter the size of a golf ball and put a teaspoon full of Ro–dex inside of that ball of peanut butter. Mix it all up very thoroughly. If you turn around and take half of that peanut butter ball and put it somewhere in a pipe – it could be 2 coffee cans put together or two 16 oz cans put together hollow like a pipe so you see straight through. Or some tile and lay down 2 together end for end flat on the ground. Or, take an old piece of pipe that you picked up off of the road or a down spout and you lay that all around where this little fellow is eating your vegetables. I can guarantee that it will take care of your problem. You'll find out that this product will kill the mouse, the shrew, the rat, the ground mole, the red squirrel, and the chipmunk. Make that pipe at least the diameter of a tennis ball. All of the things that I mentioned will go in there and eat that and never see the sunshine again.

MOSQUITOS

When you're outside you can fight those mosquitos. And there's a number of ways of solving this problem. If you're like in a wooded area or your home and there's a lot of grass, you can spray that grass with diazinon liquid in the evening. And you've unloaded a lot of mosquitos like right now.

Now when you're outside working in the garden you can turn around and you can use the Bounce that you use in your dryer. Put that around your neck, underneath your collar, in your pocket. The mosquitos cannot handle that. They'll go the other way.

I do like a bath oil – SSS Skin So Soft by Avon. I like that because you put that on your forehead or on your arms and go outside and you are mosquito free – mosquitos can not handle that SSS.

PIGEON TRAPS

Let's make a pigeon trap, real simple. Make it square or like an arc. Use hardware cloth. Any size will work. You get some wire and drill a hole in ferrells and put about a half dozen of these with spaces. Use cracked corn or bird seed in the trap. The pigeons walk in and can't get out. Make sure the ferrells use a little piece of wood at the bottom. They can push in and can't get out. Ferrells are what you use on rain spouting, very light weight. This has to set flat. Homing pigeons never land in a tree. Always where it's flat. The best time to catch a pigeon is when there is snow on the ground. The trap in the picture is 13" wide x 18" long.

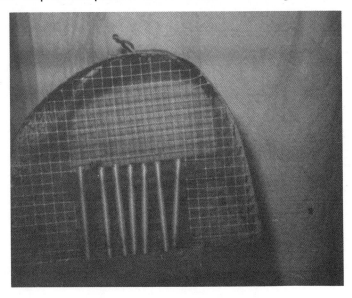

RABBITS

Let's talk about the rabbit. The rabbit always eats at a 45 degree angle and he also gets blamed for things he does not do. Now listen to what I'm telling you and read it very carefully. The rabbit cannot handle bacon grease. So if you have a little fence around your garden throw some bacon grease on the fence with a paint brush. Also get yourself a fry pan and some twine that will absorb bacon grease and melt it and put the twine all through there and hang this up like clothesline. Or you can go all the way around your garden, six inches off the ground and have it loaded with bacon grease. Now then the rabbit comes up there and smells the bacon grease and he's going to go the other way! He cannot handle bacon grease. Also you've got to realize that when it pours down rain it's going to wash the bacon grease away. So now just go out there and do it again and you'll find out that it is a pretty slick way for unloading rabbits in your garden. Also they do have a professional thing out there. It's called a hotwire for rabbits or deer. You plug it in like a farmer would use a hotline and only a couple of volts go through it. It's like

$39 or $40 and you get a wire and insulators and everything that goes with it. It works off a 110 volt. So that's another way to keep the rabbits from eating your garden.

Now another one of my fancy tricks. If you can, find binder twine that is treated with a chemical that rats and mice don't like. I soak the binder twine in used motor oil. I put this 6 inches off the ground all the way around your garden. The rabbits won't cross it. Also I turn around and I soak the binder twine that is treated with chemicals so rats and mice don't eat it and I soak this in used motor oil and I put it nose high and I've never had a deer cross that yet. That's right. So therefore, we're using something we throw away. The binder twine you'd probably get at a farm store someplace and make sure it's treated and you'll keep deer and keep rabbits from eating your garden.

RO-DEX AND YOUR GARDEN

To keep the bunnies away, mix a bottle of Tabasco sauce with two gallons of water and pour onto all the developing vegetables. Never met a rabbit with a flair for hot, spicy food!

Or, lay pieces of hose about 12" long and at least 2" diameter on the ground in your garden. Fill with human hair clippings. The human scent from the hair will keep the rabbits out.

Yet another rabbit deterrent is Vick's that has been spread onto about five inches of a protruding stick, which has been secured into the ground. The odor will keep them away. Especially successful by the lettuce patch.

RACCOONS

To avoid being pestered by these clever creatures, securely wire lids of trash cans so that if there is a raccoon in the area, it will be discouraged before raids begin.

Now let's talk about the raccoon. The raccoon can play tricks on you. Let's catch a raccoon. In the summertime all I use is 2 white marshmallows. They can see them. They can smell them. And they love them. I use a wire trap to catch them alive. Then you can relocate them, if the law permits you to do that. Also the raccoon

can not handle Pinesol soap. It's liquid. It's in a plastic bottle. Then what I do is turn around and pour a little bit of this on your plastic bags or on your garbage cans at night. They'll smell it and go the other way.

"RACCOON TRAPPER TALES"

He's Guilty

The Judge at the local courthouse called Trapper. A raccoon had made his bed outside just under the Judge's air conditioner. And, the Judge complained about the work stoppages by his employees as they watched the varmint run outside along the window sills. Trapper placed his trap using sardines as bait, but was determined the raccoon was not going to eat that lure. Trapper poked holes in the sardine can; the odor attracted the critter and he was caught. And, of course, Trapper re–used the can of sardines.

Cat Nabber

A woman called complaining her three registered pure bred cats were missing; they were no where to be found. However, a raccoon was spotted in the area. A 30 pound masked bandit ended all 27 lives of three cats, and Trapper did indeed, find cat hair in it's digestive tract. All that was left were the registration papers!

A Sad Trapper Tale

Although they appear cute and cuddly, most raccoons carry a parasitic disease. They live mostly in sewers because they find a ready supply of food there. The raccoons contract the parasite by feeding on other afflicted animals. The parasite is a round worm and is transmitted as eggs in their droppings. Their droppings are commonly found in parks, yards, wood piles, near garbage cans, and recreational areas. Nearly 70% of adult animals and 90% of their young carry the parasite. If in contact with a human, the worms can travel to the eyes and brain. A young 18 month old boy had chewed on wood chips contaminated by raccoon feces. An autopsy showed the child's body was infested with thousands of round worms.

SKUNKS

Just the name stinks! These animals are rabies carriers, don't fuss with them. They are better left alone. Carry ammonia with you when camping or at a cottage where skunks may be. Skunks find ammonia repulsive and will cower away. You can also use the gas cartridge as described for groundhogs. The poison smoke does the trick.

If you feel brave, another method is to use a long pipe with a cable or wire through it, creating a snare. Approach the skunk very slowly, slip the loop over his head and quickly lift up high enough to get his back feet off the ground. A skunk cannot spray with his hind legs off the ground.

If you are unfortu-
nate and get sprayed,
bury or burn your
clothes. The soil will
remove the odor.
Then, bathe in two
cases of tomato juice
from head to toe. Be
hopeful you're not al-
lergic to tomatoes!

SLUGS

Slugs are members of the snail family. Overnight flower damage blamed on rabbits is often the result of slugs. Potash, or ashes from your fireplace is their enemy.

To rid an area of slugs, wet the affected bed the night before and place a burlap bag or board between the rows. The burlap or board will attract them. Turn the burlap or board over the next morning; if you have slugs, they will be stuck to the underside of the board and/or burlap. To kill them, generously sprinkle table salt on them.

Another method would be to take several containers with a lid and pour beer into them. Make four to five holes in the container just above the bottom, allowing enough space to hold the beer. Place them into the flower beds. The slugs are attracted to the beer, will enter the can through the holes, get drunk, and die.

SNAKES

To keep snakes away when camping, put mothballs around your tent or cottage. Also take a bucket or gallon of diesel fuel or fuel oil; a snake will not cross over it. In the South where there are poisonous snakes, the fishermen fish at night when it's cool. They form a circle, pour diesel fuel or fuel oil around them, and they are safe from being bitten from a poisonous snake.

SNAKE TRAP

For a snake trap you can take a nylon stocking. Hang it upside down in your cellar. Prop it open a couple inches. You want that up high. Snakes want to go up high where it's nice and dry and warm. The snake will go down inside the nylon stocking and cannot get out.

You can also turn around and get a bird cage. Take out the swings and take out the sticks. Put a very small egg into the bird cage. What's going to happen? Well, snakes love eggs. It's going to go inside and eat that egg. It's going to be so fat that it can't get out. Get the smallest egg you can find on the market. It works very, very well.

There's a product out there called Snake Away. It's a fantastic product. You can put some of that in a nylon stocking. And you hang it in your cellar if you wish. Then turn around and you can put it in some jars with holes in the lid and put that on the outside. They can not handle that. Snakes will leave that area within 48 hours.

One day I got called out because someone had a pet snake about the diameter of an orange and 36–40 inches long stuck underneath the dashboard of a car. Now you can't pull that snake from underneath that dashboard, all the wires are gonna come out. And when it's cold, that snake's not gonna come down from those wires – I'll guarantee it. Now what you have to do is you have to get a light bulb and put it in the little cage with a small mouse and tie the mouse to the cage. Now the snake will smell the mouse and the light bulb will give off enough heat to attract the snake. And that's how you get a snake out from underneath the dashboard.

"TRAPPER SNAKE TALE"

I got another phone call from a lady who said she had just purchased an automobile and as she was driving home. "A snake crawled out from underneath the dashboard and underneath my leg. I stayed calm, pulled the car to the side of the road and put on my four way flashers and opened the door. When the snake got halfway out, I slammed the door and got out of my car. Pretty soon, a State Highway Patrolman came along and asked what the problem was. She told him she had a snake caught in her door and when he looked, he told her, "That's a copperhead, that's a bad one. I'll kill it."

"Well," the lady said, "I don't care what you will do with that snake, but I'm not getting back into that car. Call a tow truck and call the Trapper and ask him to meet us at the dealership." After arriving at the garage, they called me back to ask if there could be another snake in the car. I told them there possibly could be and to take a mirror and place it so they could look under the dashboard. The mirror would pick up the snake if it was there.

You guessed it. The second copperhead was underneath the dashboard. The State Highway Patrolman and mechanic were successful in getting the snake out of the car. That's just another true story and we have a lot of them.

WASPS, HORNETS, YELLOW JACKETS

Never fight them in the daytime, as half may be absent from the nest. Wait until well after dark. Fuel oil or diesel fuel will drop them fast. Use a pump type oil can or window sprayer as inexpensive applicators.

To rid an area of yellow jackets with ground nests, pour a pop bottle full of fuel oil down the hole at night and jam the neck of the bottle into it. Heap dirt around the bottle to ensure an air tight seal.

If their nest is in the wall of a building, spray Sevin dust inside and plug the hole or crack with steel wool, which they cannot chew through. Or, mix lye with caulking, and caulk the crack shut.

For hornet's nest, if one is brave, one can do as Trapper does. At night, plug the nest's single entrance at the bottom with cotton doused with diesel fuel and bag it quickly.

HINTS, REMEDIES, AND FUN PROJECTS

BEE STING REMEDIES

For a sting, put baking soda–water paste, or mud on it to draw out the poison. Or better yet, put an old penny over it. The "miracle" behind the "penny cure" is that the copper draws out the poison, so don't think a quarter will work 25 times better!

A milk soaked crust of bread left overnight under a bandage will draw out a stinger or deep splinter, or bring a boil to a head.

BIRDS

BIRD BATH

Take a tire and cut it through the middle making two halves. Plug the hole with a wood screw or cold patch. Now you have two watering dishes for dogs, cats, ducks, chickens, and birds. Best of all, it costs you nothing!

BIRD FEEDERS

HUMMINGBIRD FEEDERS

Let's talk just a little bit about the Hummingbird feeder. Hummingbirds, they absolutely fascinate me because, ya know, that is the smallest egg in the world. Now when we put our Hummingbird feeders up there, you can use any kind of solution you want to use and you will draw the Hummingbirds to it. They also like bright colors. I have a tremendous amount of calls about the ants. When you have a stem or wire holding up the Hummingbird feeder, the ants are going to come to the solution because it is sweet. How do you correct that? Well, take a pipe cleaner and put a lot of vegetable oil on the pipe cleaner and wrap that around the wire. That ant can not handle vegetable oil. Around the cups of the Hummingbird feeder you can use, again, vegetable oil. Just take your finger and go all the way around it. Also, you can turn around and use Vick's Vapor Rub or attempt some Vaseline. One of those three things is gonna work for you no matter where you live in this country.

FINCH FEEDER

Making a golden finch (wild yellow canary) feeder is quite simple. Take an empty pop bottle, turn it upside down, and put a cup hook into it. This will hold the feeder. Using a drill, make six holes for the dowel rods. Above these holes about 1 – 1/2 inches, make another hole enabling the birds to get the feed.

To fill the feeder, turn the bottle upside down, re-move the cap, and put a funnel into the spout.

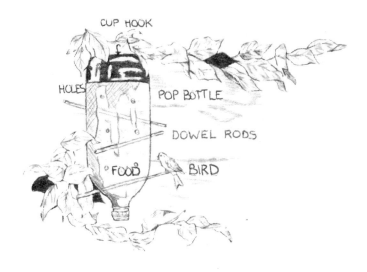

MILK CARTON BIRD FEEDER

Now I'm going to tell you how you can make a simple bird feeder out of an ordinary milk carton. Punch holes in the very tippy top of the milk carton and put string, wire, or twine through to make the hanger. Cut a hole, about the size of a golf ball, a little above the middle of two sides. These holes should be opposite each other when you are done. Now turn around and put a hole underneath each of these (the size of a stick you have). Put your stick through both holes for your perch. Now you see the birds have something to sit on while they are eating. Also cut three sides of a square up near the top of one of the sides you don't have holes in. You can use this to pour your bird seed in. That's it! You can go outside to hang it wherever you like but make sure that it is a place that the rain can't get to. Hang it somewhere so that you can see the birds come to eat and maybe you'll make a friend!

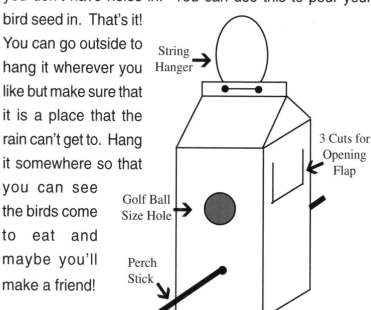

String Hanger

3 Cuts for Opening Flap

Golf Ball Size Hole

Perch Stick

BIRD HOUSE

WREN HOUSE

These two photographs show how to make a house. The top photo shows a pop can, dowel frame. The nest will be made inside the pop can which is held in place by the dowel. Hang it and enjoy the wrens!

COAL GARDEN

This is also referred to as "Depression Garden". Wash a piece of coal and lay it inside a glass container, preferably a brandy snifter or goldfish bowl. Into a pint jar, put 6 Tbsp of bluing, 6 Tbsp., of salt, 6 Tbsp. water, and 1 Tbsp. ammonia. Dissolve well and pour over the coal. Get four colors of food coloring. Place a drop of each of the four colors on top of the coal. However, be careful not to drop the colors on top of each other. This will start to grow and be very colorful. It's simple to do and fun to watch. To make a large Coal Garden, double the recipe and double the size of the glass container.

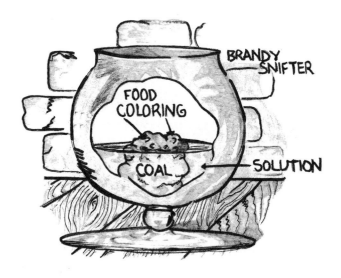

DOG'S COMFORT
AND REMEDIES

Never run a wire from a tree or the corner of a garage into your dog's chain. There is always the possibility of lightning hitting the wire and killing your dog. A wire or cable can run along the ground. Use a lead pipe or firm stick in the ground to attach your wire. This is best for two reasons. If someone unfamiliar comes into your yard, they most likely would not see the wire, and therefore, would not know how far the dog can travel. And, your dog could meet the intruder head on.

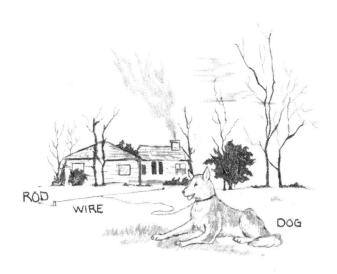

ROD
WIRE
DOG

Your dog can not only protect your home, but also your garden, especially at night when creatures tend to eat vegetables and flowers.

Self–feeders for dogs are a great way to feed him. He will only eat when he wants and the feeder design eliminates rats or mice from entering.

There is also a heating pad you can buy for your dog or cat to place in his box outside. And, the animal will not destroy it. Plug it into a house current and your animals will keep warm all winter.

DOG ITCHING

In regards to a dog that's itching and the vet can't get it because the scratch is within. There is something wrong with the dog – lacking in it's food. Always change the food. Every once in a while give it some frozen food or some cooked food or some table scraps depending on what you want to give him. I'm not in favor of giving the dog bones because you could start a problem with their stomach. Now if the dog continues to scratch and he has no fleas, then we have another problem. What you have to do is turn around and put a teaspoon full of vinegar (not white) in the drinking water. Repeat this four out of seven days. First thing you know, the vinegar heals the scratch within and the dog will quit his scratching.

FISHING TRICKS

Take a few Alka–Seltzer tablets; make a hole in the center of each one. Place your bait and a tablet on the hook. Drop it over the side of the boat into the water. When the tablet hits the water, the sizzling will cause a lot of disturbance. When you catch a fish – it will already be de– gassed!

Lay pork, beef, or liver on a post and let the sun ripen them. Using the liver for bait, you can fish tight line on the bottom with a sinker and catfish love it!

GUARANTEED BAIT

With a hypodermic needle, blow up your night crawlers; place him on your hook – he's so big, the fish can't pass him up! Especially successful with walleye fishing.

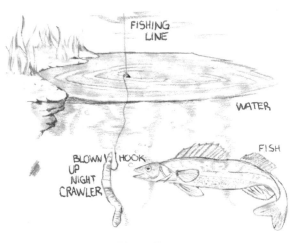

DOUGH BALL LURE

Mix one cup flour and two cups corn meal. Add two cups boiling water. Stir in 2 Tbsp. sugar and one, 3 oz. box of strawberry jello. Lower the heat and cook until the mixture is thickened. Add one Tbsp. vanilla and shape into balls. Let cool. Carry with you when fishing in a damp cloth to keep them moist. Place on hook for bait.

Also if you are cold while fishing this is a real nice trick. Take a five gallon bucket and put lots of holes in the bucket, of course I like to use a shotgun to make the holes. Then get yourself some real nice dry sand and put it in the bucket. Turn around and put lots of kerosene, like one gallon, all though the sand. Now, you can light that and the first thing you know you have a little blue flame– your hands won't be cold and you'll be nice and warm and snug fishing when it's cold or damp outside.

FROGS

IS YOUR FROG LAZY?

Place a rubber tub in your flower garden. Pour water in it and place a few rocks at the bottom. Catch a couple of frogs and place them in the tub also. The frogs will catch insects. But, how can you tell if your frog is doing the job? Take a stick, tie a string to it. On the end of the string, fray red thread. Place the red thread over top of the frogs nose. If the frog jumps onto the red thread, you have a working frog! You'll have less insects in your flower garden because you have provided a place for the frogs to eat.

FRUIT CELLAR · IN GROUND

In the Fall, when all your vegetables are ripened and picked, dig a hole large enough to hold a garbage can. Place a fairly new, not rusty, metal garbage can into the ground. Be sure the container is metal, not plastic; mice, chipmunks, and rats can eat straight through plastic – you'll be defeating your purpose. Bury the can into the soil, allowing enough room at the top for the lid to be exposed. Now, put all kinds of veggies from the garden into the can; turnips, parsnips, all varieties of squash, potatoes, and etc. Use straw or grass clippings between the layers of vegetables; however, be sure not to use grass clippings that had been sprayed with any kind of chemical. Put a bale of straw or hay over the lid to keep the veggies from freezing.

Now you have a small scale fruit cellar. This method of storage will prevent spoilage and waste.

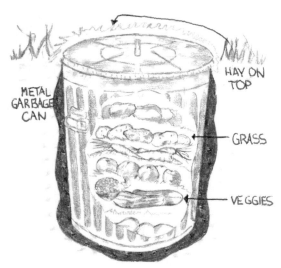

METAL GARBAGE CAN

HAY ON TOP

GRASS

VEGGIES

HOLES IN YOUR ROOF
OR HOUSE

Check the louvers on your house – at each end of the house. How can you do that? Well folks when it's a sun shiny day, you take a great big mirror (like a bathroom mirror) and you put that in the sun. Now when you're on the grass I can find every hole inside your home. That is like a $10,000 flashlight. And I'll find the holes in the roof by standing right on the ground. I don't care if it's a three story house. You can find out where the animals are getting in at. Then you get up into that attic. And once you find that out you use hardware cloth – hardware cloth – it's just a fancy word. And you tack that on the underneath of the roof vents and that stops the squirrels and the raccoons from getting in from your roof, down into your attic. Once they get in there they'll start a condominium. And the first thing you know you've got more animals up there than you can shake a stick at. Then you got big problems because the raccoon is going to tear everything up and so are the squirrels. Now we've got another problem and it didn't take much to solve it. And it's going to cost 25 cents to 50 cents just to cover the hole inside. Use staples or roof nails and hardware cloth. I want the holes the diameter of a lead pencil. That's nice and small. Right now you're protecting your house like you'd never believe.

METAL CLEANER · LIPSTICK

Any shade of lipstick is an excellent cleaner for gold, brass, sterling, copper, or other metals. Use a soft cloth to apply and another cloth or tissue to remove. Buff to a glowing lustre. The results are remarkable.

MOSQUITOS

Now the bath oil Skin So Soft by Avon, I love this product because it's liquid. What I do is I put it on a piece of cotton. Now rub the screen door screening or your bedroom screens with that SSS (Skin So Soft) and when you're done with it leave the cotton right up there also. And you'll see the flies and mosquitos come up there and go the other way. They won't come in your house because they're blocked.

ODORS

This will take the odors out of your home by doing this. What you do you go get yourself a nylon stocking – and you can do 3 or 4 or 5 or any number; then you go to the hardware store and get some calcium chloride. Now what I want you to do is put 3 or 4 cups of calcium chloride into the nylon stocking. Then hang this upstairs, downstairs, or in the basement. And; underneath the nylon stocking I want you to put a pan, a basin, or a bucket. Now what we're going to do is take all the odors out of your home. Also you can turn around and the moisture will go through the nylon stocking and into the bucket. And you're going to have a nice smelling home. You're going to take the moisture out of your home. And you didn't even spend $20.00. The calcium chloride usually comes in 40 or 50 pound bags that you get at a hardware store. And that sounds like an awful lot, but on the other hand, if you have ice or snow – you see – the calcium chloride will melt that for you. Don't put any of the solution down in your septic because you'll kill your bacteria. This is the easiest way to take an odor out of the home and take the dampness out of the home at the very same time. You can use a nylon stocking or you can take the top off of a milk carton, plastic, and put a margarine container inside that and poke lots of holes in that and put the calcium chloride in there and all the odor will go clear to the calcium chloride and then the water will be caught into the plastic jug.

BAD ODOR - KEEP THE NEWSPAPER

If you have a bad odor in your car or home, try a product called Nilodor. It comes in a 1/2 oz. bottle or aerosol can. Also try cut up newspapers. Place the shreddings into a coffee can, put the can into the refrigerator, fruit cellar, or wherever the odor is, and the paper will draw the odor out of the area. Baking soda and charcoal in the coffee can will also do the job.

ONIONS

ONION FOR COLD RELIEF REMEDY

Try this if you think you're catching a cold. Try it this year or whenever you feel it's time to catch a cold. The average house has a furnace and the furnace has a filter. You turn around and you wash the filter of your furnace or you'll put a new one in and then you put the filter back in there and what that does is clean out all the bad air that goes into your home. Now you folks listen to what I'm telling you – I mean read what I'm telling you. If you take time to turn around and take time to slice an onion or two and place it on a styrofoam container and put it on your kitchen shelf and all the bad air will go into the onion and you won't catch a cold. The onion picks up everything. The most important thing is to throw those slices of onion away on the second day. Then turn around and put an onion back out there again. A bag of onions is really economical to purchase and what you're doing is keeping yourself from catching a cold. It works like you wouldn't believe; by wife and I never have colds. And we don't do anything different than anyone else. But that onion is always on that shelf, two or three slices. If you don't use all the onion wrap it up and put it in the refrigerator and bring it back out.

Now another thing that I tried out – I have an onion on the garage floor with some kerosene along side of it and I took a bite of that onion in the morning and it tastes like kerosene!! Also, that tells me that the onion draws all of that bad air – whatever is in your home. So you have to remember that I get all kinds of phone calls and it's been doing a very good job through the area and all over the country.

ONIONS ALSO WORK ON ANIMALS

Also I had a farmer call me and he had a calf that was down. That baby calf wasn't doing too good and wasn't eating. It was down for two solid days. When I got the phone call I said to him you've got to get the cobwebs out of the calf's head and what I want you to do is slice 4 or 5 onions and lay it on each side of the baby calf, regardless of which way that calf turns his head, it has to smell the onions. I don't care what kind you get just get them. He called back 4 or 5 days later and said, "Trapper, I can't believe it." He said, "I went to the barn on the third day and that calf was standing up and ready to eat." So there's so much things so good for that onion it's unbelievable besides cooking it or eating it raw.

"TRAPPER REMEDY TALE"

Now I had a lady call who had one 6 year old child in bed with the flu and 5 children plus the mother and father. I said to her to put slices of onion out there and every day for 4 days I wanted her to throw the onion away and put a fresh onion out there. She called back when I asked her to and there's a young lady who could tell her story – not one of those folks in that family got the flu. It works, I have a lot of faith in it, I love that onion and I eat as much of it as I can and I turn around and keep some on my shelf. All through the Fall, especially.

PREDICTING THE WEATHER

How would you like to know what the weather is going to be? We do this activity on Christmas Eve and read it on January 6. Here is the procedure. Slice 6 onions and that will give you 12 halves. Get an empty egg carton and there are 12 holes. These onions will stand for 12 the months. Put each half onion in each hole of the egg carton. Take out a calendar and cut out the months or write each month out on a small piece of paper. Attach each month to a toothpick. Start with January and put a teaspoon of table salt on each onion. You will read this on January 6th. Whatever months the salt has disappeared will be the wet months of the year. Then, we're going to set this by a favorite window so some of the air can get to the onions.

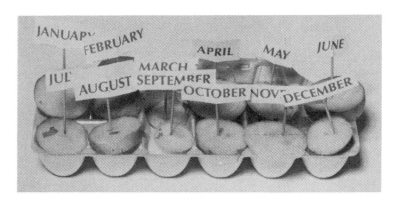

RAIN, FOG, OR SNOW?

Look at the sky at night. You'll view the moon from different angles. Notice a ring around the moon. If the moon is full, and you see stars around the moon, count the stars. Each star represents a day. So, if you are outside tonight and see a full moon with a ring around it, and around the moon there are five stars, the fifth day will be the day it rains. Keep track to check your accuracy.

If it rains on Easter Sunday, it will rain seven Sundays in a row.

For every day of fog in August, there will be a day of snow the next winter.

And to predict what kind of winter we'll have, observe mother nature. Hornets' nests close to the ground indicate a cold winter. When a hornet digs a hole in the ground, he's going "South for the winter" resulting in sub–zero temperatures and severe cold. If the hornets' nest are up in the tree tops and in the eaves of two–story houses, the winter will be mild, however, there will be more snowfall.

Ant hills as high as your knees, nuts with heavy coats, and field corn with thick husks are also sure signs of a cold winter.

Trapper has been right on target eight out of ten times in the past four years with his weather predictions.

POISON IVY

Boil a quart of rock salt in a gallon of water until you have created a super saturated brine. Place the solution in a sprinkling can and use to "water" the ivy. The leaves will brown the next day.

Never burn a fire around poison ivy or burn the dead ivy plants. Smoke carries the ivy's irritating oil and can get into your lungs which can develop into poison ivy of the stomach, resulting in serious illness or even death.

Also, to cure poison ivy, rub the inside of a banana peel gently on the poison ivy.

POTATOES
THEIR REMARKABLE MAGIC !

Well I have a lot of faith in a potato. I eat a raw potato every morning before breakfast. I like to have the potato about the size of a golf ball. And, I eat the peelings and all. Now there's so many things in that potato that are so good for us if your system can handle it. You folks are going to feel better. There's no question about it. We're taking medicines and we don't even know what we're taking and we do know about this good old fashioned potato. I like the red potato, but that's just my preference. They seem to be juicier. I buy them at the store. Around Ohio here, they have the potatoes on the shelf already sorted for you.

Now that potato, folks, will help you like you never believe, like I said if your system can handle it. There's one lady who was taking 5 pills, and she's not taking any pills anymore. She's getting along very nicely by eating a potato. There's another lady that could hardly walk. She was getting all stoved up and crippled up and couldn't drive her car anymore. By that lady eating a potato she's now driving her car again at 77 years of age. Now there's another man who is now milking his cows and he's hung the walker up. He was on a walker, hung the walker up in the garage and now be's back out doing his chores again and he's walking pretty normal.

There's another man that had cancer of the liver and he heard me speak one time and when he went to the doctor because he was bloated, had a lot of indigestion and he had a lot of air. He heard me speak and he said, "I've got to try that potato to see what's going on here, see if I can get this body straightened around." And, would you believe that he called me back one day and he said, "Boy, Trapper, that potato is fantastic. It's unloaded all my gas and all of my heartburn and I don't have no more air." Now the cancer is all the way down to a golf ball size." Maybe soon you'll find out some day that there's stuff in that potato that's going to help cure our cancer. I feel it's just around the corner. The doctors or whoever does all that scientific stuff are going to find that out. This man is doing so good he even took a trip away and what did he do? He took ten pounds of potatoes with him so he wouldn't run out. I came back from Canada not too long ago and we took our potatoes with us also. We were only up there a couple of days but the potatoes just have so many things in there that are excellent for our system, if your system can handle it.

I deliberately ate a lot of spaghetti one night. A lot of spaghetti and a lot of meatballs. I had heartburn and bloating. Ordinarily you would take something to unload that problem from your medicine cabinet. What did I do? I went and ate a raw potato. A raw potato, peeling and all. In twenty minutes my indigestion was completely gone. Try it folks, it might really really help you out. I have a lot of faith in the potato.

HEADACHE RELIEF

Have a terrific headache and nothing seems to relieve the pain? Cut a potato into thin slices. Place the slices over your forehead and lay down for ten minutes. The iron and potassium do the trick. Does the job on burns too! And, potatoes are cheaper than ointments or aspirin.

SANDBOX AND SWING
MAKE YOUR OWN

You can make a swing for a child from a tire. Tie a rope around it and hang it from a tree.

If you can get a big tractor tire, use it to make a sand box. Fill the center with sand, and the children will sit around on the tire. Secure a stick with a rubber ball on the end into the center of the sand and place a tarp over it. (The rubber ball will not allow the stick to puncture through the tarp). Extend the four corners out over the tire, attaching a stick with a rubber ball to each corner, and secure into the ground outside the tire. The tarp will keep the sand dry and the cats out, too!

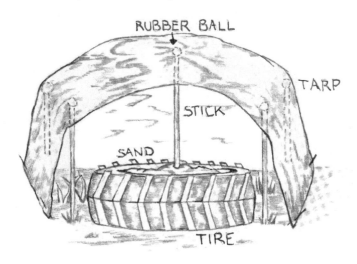

"SKIN SO SOFT"
MANY HOUSEHOLD USES

SSS by Avon, is a bath oil and after shower moisturizer. It can be used to remove makeup and it's great tanning oil. Also can be used as a hot oil treatment to soften cuticles and a massage oil for tired muscles. It's an insect repellent for people as well as pets, and it helps relieve the itching caused by insect bites and dry skin. Especially effective to prevent mosquito bites when rubbed on arms, forehead, ankles, etc. Do not dilute.

Mix five parts water to one part Skin So Soft and mist on show animals. Brush into their fur. Their coats will gleem and the insects will stay away.

SSS is a good wood cleaner and conditioner for natural wood. It removes glue and gum left from price tags and labels from glass, metal and most plastics.

It will also clean off tape marks left from bandages on skin. It will remove ink from skin and most vinyl surfaces, also painted surfaces.

Painting something? Use SSS to remove paint from hands, rather than turpentine.

It also cleans heavy oil and grease from skin and

non–porous surfaces. Use it to remove soap scum from shower doors, shower curtains, windows and bathroom and kitchen fixtures. It will also remove the lime and hard water deposits from the fixtures, tile, shower doors, and windows.

Having trouble removing tar spots from car finishes? SSS will do the job without damage to the paint.

SORE MUSCLES AND SPRAINS

HORSE LINIMENT FOR HUMANS!

Look for the bottle with the picture of the horse (Absorbine Veterinary Liniment) and you'll have the best cure for sore muscles and arthritis. Or, dice two bulbs of garlic into a pint of rubbing alcohol. Ferment for one day; rub on arthritic areas three or four times a day.

MULLEN WEED REMEDY

By summertime, Mullen weed is five to six feet high, with leaves 19 inches long and five inches wide. Boil the weed in vinegar for two minutes. Let cool. Wrap the leaf around the sprained area, (ankle, wrist, or other joint), and the swelling will go down.

SWEAT IN THE SUMMER

If you work outdoors often in the summertime and sweat badly, you need to cool off. Pump water out of the well, and run the cold water onto your wrists. This method will cool you off very quickly. Also, if you are outside and get gaulled between the legs, get two to three elderberry leaves, and put them in your pants pocket. The chemistry in the leaves will protect you and solve your problem.

Overheated outside? Place a large piece of sliced onion in your shoes! Wear light colored socks.

TREE IN YOUR REFRIGERATOR

Would you like to start a tree in your refrigerator? You heard me – a tree in the refrigerator! In the Fall all the nuts come down. I don't care what kind of nuts out there, walnut, hickory, butternut, acorn, buckeye, you name it, we'll sprout it. You take a mayonnaise jar and you put holes in the lid. A good half a dozen holes at least the size of a pencil. Then you get some peat moss and you dampen the peat moss. Then you put a layer of nuts in the bottom of the peat moss. Then you use some more peat moss, dampened, and you put that on top of those nuts. Now you can go all the way to the top of the jar. I don't care if you use a pint jar, a quart jar, and then you put the lid on it. Set this clear at the back of your refrigerator. Don't pull it out until the end of April. You'll find out that every nut sprouts. In the refrigerator! All winter! Then you take it out at the end of April or the first week of May and you put this in flower pots. Then you set the flower pots outside with the nuts already sprouting. And you bring it back in and you take it out until you get it acclimated with your weather. How about this! You started your tree in your refrigerator. Now you have trees to share with your neighbors and it didn't cost anything.

UDDER CREAM

REDEX UDDER CREAM

There's a beautiful product out there called udder cream. I think so much of this product. It's just helping people throughout all of our states. There are just so many things that this will do for you. How about taking care of chapped hands? How about taking care of sores on your split fingers? How about taking care of sunburn? How about taking care of just about any blemish there is on your skin? It moistens, it smells so good, it's pure white. You'll want to carry this around with you. Women take a container of this and put it in their purse. You know, I've had people tell me already it's taken care of hemorrhoids and also taken care of bed sores. You're going to like it. Here's a toll free number: 1-800-345-7339. I don't think there's a product out there like it. It is made in Salem, Ohio. Always remember that. Salem, Ohio, and it's unloading the chapped hands for the people that work out there like contractors, electrical workers and telephone men. Try it folks, you're going to love it.

WART REMOVAL

Place a piece of raw bacon under a bandage, piece of tape, or gauze over the wart. Or use iodine; the wart will be gone in due time.

WILDLIFE IDENTIFICATION QUIZ

OHIO DEPARTMENT OF NATURAL RESOURCES

DIVISION OF WILDLIFE

Mammal Tracks and Trails

Identify the tracks of the animals shown on the following pages, and fill the empty circles with the correct number. The tracks are not drawn to scale.

1. Cottontail Rabbit
2. Raccoon
3. Muskrat
4. Woodchuck
5. Mink
6. Long Tail Weasel
7. Beaver
8. Bobcat
9. Dog
10. Gray Squirrel
11. Red Fox
12. Opossum
13. Striped Skunk
14. Chipmunk
15. White-Tailed Deer

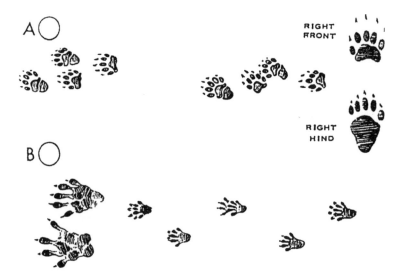

C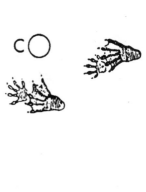

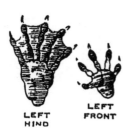

LEFT
HIND

LEFT
FRONT

D

E

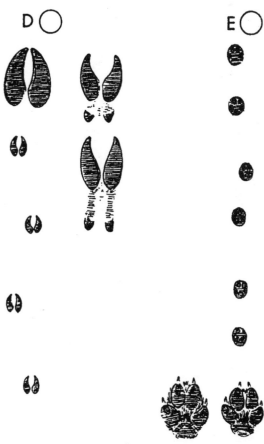

FRONT   HIND

139

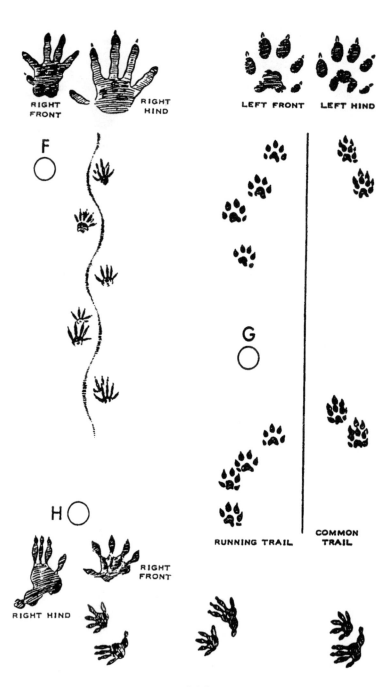

RIGHT FRONT RIGHT HIND

LEFT FRONT LEFT HIND

F

G

RUNNING TRAIL COMMON TRAIL

H

RIGHT FRONT

RIGHT HIND

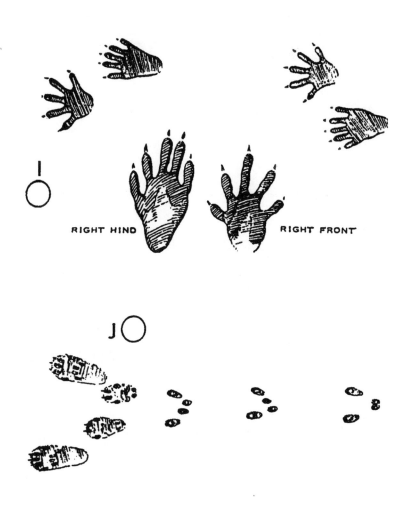

RIGHT HIND

RIGHT FRONT

WILDLIFE RULES & REGULATIONS

OHIO DEPARTMENT OF NATURAL RESOURCES
DIVISION OF WILDLIFE

PUBLICATION 327 (R983)

Live-Trapping Wild Animals in Villages or Cities

In any incorporated village or city wherein the hunting of game is unlawful, any person can live-trap non-migratory wild birds or wild mammals when such birds or mammals have become a nuisance. Such live-trapping must be in accordance with the following provisions:

1. Only those live traps which will not cause death or injury to persons or domestic or wild animals may be used.

2. A durable waterproof tag bearing the name and address of the user in English letters must be attached to each live trap.

3. Live-trapped animals must be released outside of the incorporated village or city within 24 hours of the time of capture.

4. Any person wishing to live-trap on lands of another must first have written permission from the landowner or the landowner's authorized agent.

5. It is unlawful to sell (except as provided below), use, mistreat, injure, or give to another person, any wild bird or wild mammal live-trapped for removal from an incorporated village or city.

6. Wild mammals may be trapped within the limits of a city by persons having a special permit issued by the Division of Wildlife. Persons possessing such a permit may charge a nominal fee for removal of the animal or they may sell fur bearing animals taken under this permit at any time to Ohio residents. However, they cannot charge for the removal of a furbearer and then sell that furbearer. Persons having such permits must keep current records of when and to whom sales are made and submit a report to the Division of Wildlife by May 15 of each year.

Wire live traps for mammals and birds are manufactured by several companies and can be purchased or ordered through retail stores. Plans for building wood box traps are shown for those who decide to build their own live traps. As shown, the box trap is designed for live-trapping rabbits. It can also be used for trapping opossums and skunks. For live-trapping squirrels, the box trap can be modified by substituting 1/4" mesh hardware cloth for the rear wood partition.

TRAPPER LAUGHS & GIGGLES

WHAT AN ODOR!

This man was going down the highway and he picked up this lady because she was broke down. She got into his vehicle and as they were riding to the repair shop, the man asked her what she had on that smelled so good. "Oh," she said, "that is very expensive perfume that costs $1,500 an ounce." He said, "I have never smelled anything like that before, it smells really good!" As they were driving down the road, they were chewing the fat when all of a sudden she smelled something very, very bad. "What in the world is that?", she asked. He said, "It's just pork and beans, three cans for a dollar."

STUBBORN AS A MULE

This farmer had a mule and that mule was always getting away. And he could never keep a halter on it. Well, a neighbor pulls into his driveway and he says "Si, will you go over and get that mule out of my garden! He's stomping everything down." So, Si went over and got the old mule and brought it home. He stuck it back outside and went in the house. When he came back out to sit on his porch, a lady came knocking at the door. She says, " Ya know I'm a new neighbor and they tell me that's your mule in my front yard. It's got all kinds of footprints all though the grass! This is terrible! Get that mule out of that yard!" So Si said, "Alright, I'll go ahead over there and get that mule. I'm sorry. It won't happen again." So Si goes to the mule and says, "By Golly, I'll fix you mule!" So he turned around and he backed the mule up to a tree and he tied his tail around the tree. Well, wouldn't you know, some lady pulled in there all mad and all bent out of shape. Si says, "What's the matter?" "Well, Listen here! Listen here! Listen here! That, that, that mule over there has got his tail tied around that tree," she says. "Well," he said, "I'll tell you something ma'am." Si said, "Listen here, that mule sawed his halter off, he's been in the garden and in the grass and I'll be darned if that mule will pull his tail off. He'll be right there in the morning."

CHIMNEY HEAD

A friend of mine picked up a man. He asked him not to smoke in this truck. The man said, "Let me out at the next crossroad." My friend said "If the good Lord wanted you to smoke he would have put a chimney on your head."

QUARTER A HUG

I went to a lady's house to solve a problem for her. She was in her eighties and very grateful. We settled up, then I gave her a great big hug. I said, "I charge a quarter for this hug." She handed me a dollar and said, "I want a dollar's worth!"

COLD BIRD

A minister had a parrot. Every time people came to visit, the parrot would swear. So he put the parrot in the freezer for 10 minutes to straighten him out. The parrot did it again and the minister put him back in the freezer for 20 minutes this time. When he took him out and put him on his perch, the parrot said, "I only swore a little bit, I wonder what happened to the turkey, he's been in there for 12 months!"

A TRUE TRAPPER STORY

A lady listens to my show every week on WKBN 570 AM that begins at 6:00 a.m. on Saturday. She said to me, " I have a large family and I don't want to wake them up. So, I turn on the radio and put it in my bed under the covers. Then it's just you and me."

BESSIE THE HEIFER

1) My daddy gave a calf to me
>> for a Christmas present once.
> I picked a little heifer
>> 'cause both of us were runts.
> She never had no sense
>> but she grew up all right somehow.
> When it came to givin' milk,
>> she was an educated cow!

Chorus:
> Bessie, the heifer, the queen
>> of all the cows
> She gave more milk than any law allows
> In the morning she gave pasteurized
>> at night she gave homogenized
> Bessie, the heifer, the queen of all the cows.

2) I took her to the county fair
   to try to win a prize.
   She knew what was goin' on
   I saw it in her eyes.
   The contest made her nervous
   and she tried so hard to please,
   That when I tried to milk her
   All I got was cottage cheese!

Chorus:

3) I planted me a tater patch
   to earn some extra dough,
   To take a short vacation
   with some city folks I know.
   But no one else would milk the cow
   no matter how I'd nag
   So Pa took my vacation,
   leaving me to hold the bag.

Chorus:

NDC012710-6025-1

DIRECTIONS FOR USE

CAUTION: Wash udder and teat parts thoroughly with clean water and soap before each milking to avoid contamination of milk. Use clean individual towels for this purpose. Apply to the udder after each milking, massaging into the skin. For teat cracks apply in sufficient quantity to fill crack and cover surrounding area. Apply uniformly to chafed area and bruises to maintain skin suppleness.

For aid in softening swollen udders following calving, apply liberally twice daily with gentle massage.

May be used for chapped or chafed skin. Do not use in or near eyes.

A Protective Coating, Useful for Treatment of Chapped Teats and as an Aid for Keeping Skin Soft and Supple.

GREASELESS • STAINLESS

Enriched with Lanolin and Allantoin
MANUFACTURED BY

CONTAINS: Allantoin, Dimethicone, Lanolin, and Propylene Glycol in an Emollient Base.

WARNING: Do not use on parts affected with cow pox, as such use may contribute to the spread of the infection. Thoroughly wash treated udder and teats with clean water and soap before each milking to avoid contamination of milk. Use clean individual towels for this purpose.

CAUTION
KEEP THIS AND ALL MEDICINES OUT OF CHILDREN'S REACH.

NET WT. 10 OZ.

REDEX INDUSTRIES INC •   • SALEM, OHIO 44460   1-800-345-7339

Bill Kennedy Sr.
President

1176 Salem Parkway • Salem, OH • 44460
(216) 332-9800 • FAX (216) 332-1061

ORDER FORM

Please send me _____ copies of THE FRIENDLY TRAPPER for $10.00 plus $4.00 postage and handling per book ordered for U.S. Mailing. ($6.00 for Canada) **Make checks payable to and mail to:**

TRAPPER PUBLICATIONS

P.O. Box 423

Canfield, OH 44406-0423

Phone: 216-549-2010

Mail Books to:

NAME_____

ADDRESS_____

CITY_____ STATE_____ ZIP_____

This book is a perfect gift for any home owner. To order extra copies for your friends or neighbors, please use the above Order Forms. Photo copies of these Order Forms are acceptable.

NOTES